T0328664

Cambridge Elements ≡

Elements in Public Policy
edited by
M. Ramesh
National University of Singapore (NUS)
Michael Howlett
Simon Fraser University, British Columbia
Xun WU
Hong Kong University of Science and Technology (Guangzhou)
Judith Clifton
University of Cantabria
Eduardo Araral
National University of Singapore (NUS)

DESIGNING BEHAVIOURAL INSIGHTS FOR POLICY

Processes, Capacities and Institutions

Ishani Mukherjee
Singapore Management University

Assel Mussagulova
The University of Sydney

CAMBRIDGE
UNIVERSITY PRESS

Shaftesbury Road, Cambridge CB2 8EA, United Kingdom

One Liberty Plaza, 20th Floor, New York, NY 10006, USA

477 Williamstown Road, Port Melbourne, VIC 3207, Australia

314–321, 3rd Floor, Plot 3, Splendor Forum, Jasola District Centre,
New Delhi – 110025, India

103 Penang Road, #05–06/07, Visioncrest Commercial, Singapore 238467

Cambridge University Press is part of Cambridge University Press & Assessment,
a department of the University of Cambridge.

We share the University's mission to contribute to society through the pursuit of
education, learning and research at the highest international levels of excellence.

www.cambridge.org
Information on this title: www.cambridge.org/9781009500364

DOI: 10.1017/9781009264464

First published 2024

A catalogue record for this publication is available from the British Library.

ISBN 978-1-009-50036-4 Hardback
ISBN 978-1-009-26447-1 Paperback
ISSN 2398-4058 (online)
ISSN 2514-3565 (print)

Designing Behavioural Insights for Policy Processes, Capacities and Institutions

Elements in Public Policy

DOI: 10.1017/9781009264464
First published online: April 2024

Ishani Mukherjee
Singapore Management University

Assel Mussagulova
The University of Sydney

Author for correspondence: Ishani Mukherjee, ishanim@smu.edu.sg

Abstract: The diversity of knowledge surrounding behavioural insights (BI) means in the policy sciences, although visible, remains under-theorised with scant comparative and generalisable explorations of the procedural prerequisites for their effective design, as both stand-alone tools and part of dedicated policy 'toolkits'. While comparative analyses of the content of BI tools have proliferated, the knowledge gap regarding the procedural needs of BI policy design is growing recognisably as the range of BI responses grows in practice, necessitating specific capabilities, processes and institutional frameworks to be in place for their design. This Element draws on the literature on policy design and innovation adoption to explore the administrative, institutional and capacity endowments of governments for the successful and appropriate integration of BI in existing policy frameworks. Further, this Element presents three illustrative cases with respect to their experience of essential procedural endowments facilitating the effective integration of BI in policy design.

Keywords: behavioural public policy, policy design, procedural tools, behavioural insights, nudges

ISBNs: 9781009500364 (HB), 9781009264471 (PB), 9781009264464 (OC)
ISSNs: 2398-4058 (online), 2514-3565 (print)

Contents

1 Introduction

1.1 Behavioural Insights as a Policy 'Toolkit'

Behavioural insights (BI) are becoming increasingly omnipresent in the public policy and administration landscapes of many countries around the world. Since the publication of Thaler and Sunstein's (2009) seminal text on the use of psychological insights to influence behaviour and achieve policy goals, several national governments have been experiencing a new behavioural turn, while others have built on already-existing frameworks for incorporating policy tools of moral suasion into existing regulatory toolkits. Evidence abounds, in both cases, of the adoption of BI for policy-making in some of the most important aspects of public life, such as health care, education, the environment, transport and security.

Behavioural insights in this regard are broadly defined as the collection of approaches for designing public policy, which incorporates evidence about human psychology into policy instrument formulation (Hallsworth & Kirkman, 2020). As such, BI can be situated at the micro-level of policy design wherein policy instrument settings and calibrations are adjusted based on behavioural evidence (e.g. modifying the frequency and form of tax reminders), and also at the operational level of policy programmes (e.g. designing a public health programme on healthy eating) (Ruggeri, 2018). The BI approach recognises that people are not entirely rational agents, and their decision-making process is subject to various cognitive biases and heuristics. Behavioural insight-based policy interventions are usually implemented by altering the 'choice architecture', or the way in which policy choices are presented to the citizens whose behaviour the government is looking to change. Nudges, for example, are designed to direct citizens to a particular decision through the use of defaults, where the desired decision is the default one. However, BI is not limited to nudging designs and may take the form of commitment devices or alternative framing to encourage specific action or non-action (Gopalan & Pirog, 2017). More cognitive forms of nudges, or 'thinks', have also been widely employed wherein the targeted behaviour change is meant to be long-term, relying on individuals' own deliberation and thought processes (John et al., 2020). The growing BI 'toolkit' in policy design thus spans a range of responses that, in turn, necessitate specific capabilities, procedures and institutional frameworks to be in place for their design.

However, a comparative discussion of the procedural considerations of BI tool design is currently lacking, with a few notable exceptions (Lunn, 2012; OECD, 2017; Whitehead et al., 2017). Some forays into the administrative structure of BI tools have been made recently, and while this literature remains mostly scattered, they point to several patterns of BI tool design that can contribute to broad policy instrument and policy formulation studies, for example, the governance resources of organisation (both substantive and procedural) that these tools rely on. The organisational configuration of BI policy design in countries like the United Kingdom, for instance, manifests itself through dedicated BI units located at the heart of the government. Other governments rely on a more networked approach with mobile teams of BI experts across ministries and agencies. Finally, some countries utilise a more flexible, ad-hoc format of BI input, where behavioural insights are used for specific projects and initiatives, and experts (both internal and external) are involved on a contractual basis (Afif et al., 2019; Feitsma, 2018, 2019; Mukherjee & Giest, 2020). The empirical evidence on such patterns, while disjointed, suggests that there is no single favoured approach to designing BI tools, or to integrating them into existing policy toolkits.

1.2 The Evolution of Behavioural Insights (BI) within the Policy Design and Formulation Literatures

Behavioural insight intervention within the policy design literature is a vibrant yet under-theorised area of discourse, even though it has been explored in other research domains pertaining to policy, such as policy mechanisms (Capano & Howlett, 2020); epistemic communities (Simons & Schniedermann, 2021; Weible, 2018); policy transfer (Ball & Feitsma, 2020); and comparative studies (Jones et al., 2013; Whitehead et al., 2019), among others. The proliferation of BI policy tools has been especially prominent, for example, during the pandemic era, as the global movement to scale up community behaviours quickly and critically for supporting public health has led to unique interactions between novel BI interventions and existing or more traditional health policy instruments. Other sectors, such as environmental and climate policy, have also seen a marked increase in the use of BI mechanisms to enhance or supplement regulatory or incentive-based policy instruments (Carlsson et al., 2021; Gravert & Shreedhar, 2022).

Studies of these developments in the area of BI policy research, beyond their application, have also burgeoned over the last decade. Most of this scholarship retains a clear emphasis on the substantive content and contributions of BI interventions, and their place and role in the multi-instrument 'toolkits' that governments design during times of relative stability, as well as during times of crisis. There is agreement in the policy sciences literature that policy design can be more or less systematic in attempting to match policy ends and means in a logical fashion. In all cases, formulators make assumptions about the capabilities of policy tools and their ability to achieve predictable policy outcomes (Capano, 2020; Capano & Engeli, 2022; Howlett et al., 2020; Howlett & Leong, 2022). Usually, the choice of instruments is based on either ideological premises or the empirically informed perception of how different categories of instruments can engage and modify the behaviour of policy targets (Schneider & Ingram, 1990). The unique capabilities of different classes of policy instruments and their resulting ability to achieve policy goals involve a consideration of how sets of actors behave, implicitly or explicitly, through the deployment of tools to deliver specific kinds of responses on the part of their intended targets. This is the case even though policy-makers may not always be familiar with a causal way of thinking (at least, they may not always be aware that they activate certain behaviours when implementing their chosen policy design).

The discussion regarding the need to study this underlying behavioural logic of design choice has been recently invigorated in the policy sciences (Capano & Howlett, 2020). More active engagement with the literature on behavioural policy tools, their formulation and deployment, through the perspective of traditional policy instrument studies, can help to address this emerging research agenda and to move beyond any deterministic stance regarding how particular behaviours can arise only by deploying particular policy instruments.

1.2.1 BI Interactions in Multilevel Portfolios as Calibrations, Tools and Programmes

The most specific level of policy design, that of tool settings and calibrations – or the on-the-ground considerations for implementing policy tools – has generally evaded focused theorisation in the policy design literature (Sewerin et al., 2022). At the same time, this is typically also the main operational venue for behavioural insights in public policy, and despite the evolving richness of this literature, it has yet to engage with broader policy instruments and policy design.

In the developing body of work on policy design of the last two decades, one assumption that has remained somewhat constant is the relationship between policy targets and policy instruments. Notions of policy target incentives, compliance and rationality are mostly taken as a given in discussions of various policy tools and the civic reactions they are meant to enable. The vast heterogeneity of policy 'taker' and policy 'maker' behaviours, as reflected through empirical and contextual realities, has only been recently addressed in policy design studies (Capano & Engeli, 2022; Capano & Howlett, 2020; Howlett et al., 2020). Most examples of this heterogeneity have been visible at the level of on-the-ground policy implementation choices, rather than at the broader level of policy abstraction. For example, at the level of policy calibrations, those directly in charge of implementation (such as street-level bureaucrats) can also be active policy formulators, influencing, supplementing and often also challenging the design of policy instruments (Cohen & Aviram, 2021). However, bridging such empirical lessons from policy tool implementation with the theoretical understanding of on-the-ground tool calibrations remains in its nascent stages, and a focus on behavioural insights provides a rich venue for seeding such connections.

With multiple instrument components being assembled in crisis-response policy packages for critical situations such as the recent COVID-19 pandemic, there is a heightened need for greater recognition of how instruments are created to work together to bring about a mix of desired social behaviours at the operation level (Capano & Howlett, 2020). This area of research, however, has been mostly ascribed to the 'classic' works on policy instrument choice, which retained a deliberate focus on the behavioural outcomes of policy design (Howlett et al., 2009). Early notable efforts to study the behavioural impact of specific tools included work on finding ways to better categorise and 'genericise' policy tool efforts to evaluate their impact and effect on policy outcomes and efforts to develop models of tool use and to explain patterns found in their use (Bemelmans-Videc et al., 2011; Hood, 2007; Salamon 2000; Schneider & Ingram, 1990). Schneider and Ingram (1990), for example, proposed a seminal typology of policy instruments based on common underlying behavioural assumptions, while Salamon (2000) emphasised the multidimensionality of instruments. Based on this insight, Christopher Hood generated a major work on the subject (Hood, 2007) that received much international attention. Hood's discussion was directly influenced by detailed studies of policy implementation processes and involved a resource-based categorisation scheme for policy instruments. Through this categorisation, he argued that governments have at their disposal predominantly four resources with which to impact behavioural outcomes – nodality (meaning the resource that exists in the form of sharing knowledge, information and, increasingly, public messaging and mechanisms to increase public awareness); authority (legal power); treasure (financial assets); and organisation (by way of public sector management and partnerships with relevant non-state stakeholders) (or 'NATO'). Schneider and Ingram's (1990) instruments perspective, on the other hand, is based on the notion that policy instruments activate specific policy actor tendencies, which lead to predictable behavioural changes on the part of policy targets and ultimately result in foreseeable policy outcomes. Through these developments, it was understood that bringing out modifications in the behaviour of target populations could be viewed as the central goal of policy instrument design and its subsequent deployment through policy programmes (Howlett, 2018). More recent comparative analyses of these various policy instrument categorisation efforts suggest that resource-based (such as Hood's) and behaviour-based (such as Schneider and Ingram's) classifications are fundamentally different in terms of their design logic (Capano & Engeli, 2021). However, empirical studies on micro-level instrument operations that are behaviourally based contextualise how governance resources and behavioural drivers may blend. As surmised by Capano and Engeli (2021), such micro-perspectives can 'reveal the similarities and differences in the content, ways of delivery and rules of accountability of the policy instruments themselves', and 'without the inclusion of the operative aspect, the typology tradition in policy instrument research is likely to become infertile' (16).

This statement is made particularly pertinent in lessons emerging about policy design in response to the COVID-19 pandemic, with the realisation that policy targets can exhibit a wide range of behaviours in response to policy initiatives that are not limited to simple hedonic calculations of self-maximisation. While the surge of behavioural insights penetrating the social sciences has questioned traditional utilitarian assumptions of perfectly informed risk–benefit assessments of individuals, these assumptions still permeate much of the policy design literature with an understanding of policy target compliance (Howlett, 2018; Oliver, 2015; Thaler & Sunstein, 2009). Designing programmes according to the incentives and disincentives triggered by the deployment of policy instruments is still the main consideration of the majority of policy design literature. Calling for a transition beyond the traditional 'compliance-deterrence' logics of policy design, Howlett (2018) argues that 'most behaviorally inspired analyses "subjects" are still seen to be motivated to promote pleasure and to avoid pain and to do so in an essentially calculating "cost–benefit" fashion when confronted by the choice of rewards or penalties associated with whether or not they comply with government measures' (105; Steg et al., 2014). Many authors have alluded to the complexity that is inherent in understanding the compliance-related behaviours of policy targets during the creation of policy instruments, which go beyond the analysis of rational economic cost and engender other socio-cultural and psychological considerations such as appropriateness, legitimacy and blame-avoidance (Knetsch, 2012; Wan et al., 2015).

Therefore, the explicit focus on behavioural change and the embedded impact of individual decisions within social contexts has gradually taken centre-stage in public policy discourses, but with limited discussion on how it is changing the work of policy design. While the concept of 'nudges' and related behavioural instruments (Thaler & Sunstein, 2009) have risen to fame over the last two decades, the focus on targeting individual behaviours with policy interventions has been an integral part of government policy-making for far longer. For example, in Singapore the incorporation of behavioural science into policy formulation has taken place since the 1960s in sectors ranging from the environment (for example, the 'Keep Singapore Clean' public sanitation campaign of 1968, which used social signalling) to social policy (such as the nationalisation of default enrolment into organ donation in 2009; Galizzi, 2017). What remains elusive is a discussion on how this focus on behaviour has shaped organisational and operational choices made within government about policy design, and hence the focus of this Element.

Acknowledging the diversity of BI tools is perhaps the first step towards drawing generalisable lessons about the contributions they make in traditional policy toolkits and how they shape the task of policy design. While behavioural policy scholars have surmised that 'all tools are informational now' (John, 2013, 605), and fundamental to 'recalibrating the instruments of state' (John, 2013, 616), they also express that not every behavioural intervention is a simple heuristic-modifying nudge (Howlett, 2018). Behavioural insight mechanisms beyond pure nudges have now proliferated into a range of tools that incorporate cognitive, participatory and discursive elements – such as 'system-2 nudges', 'nudge plus', 'boosts' and 'thinks' – each offering different ways to support the operation of policy designs and designing based on behavioural insights (Moseley, 2020). Importantly, these various tools require different governance resources to be deployed for their design during policy formulators.

Within this diversity, efforts to first categorise and classify different BI tools remain at a nascent stage and the inherent ambiguities in the policy-relevant literature on BI mechanisms remain stark. In parallel, policy design research and studies on policy instruments are increasingly conscious of the limitations of one-size-fits-all rational instrument decisions and support frameworks of analysis that are sensitive and embedded within contextual factors. This is especially the case as nudging is understood as only one of many efforts with the aim of comprehending the complexity of community behaviours such as co-production and cognitive deliberation, which vary when dealing with complex public problems such as pandemics (Howlett, 2018; Strassheim & Beck, 2019). What we witness is thus a burgeoning yet unguided body of BI policy literature and a parallel call in the policy design literature for a more nuanced discussion of rationality within policy design studies, with the implied synergy of these two streams yet to be explored.

1.3 A Framework for BI Policy Design

The modern discourse on behavioural public policy presents four main theses related to the evolution of BI tools. Firstly, and most encompassing, is that behavioural policy evidence strongly suggests that there is more than one class of BI policy interventions that infuse behavioural notions (dominated by ideas of automatic individual actions guided by mental heuristics, or 'nudges') with more varied cognitive considerations (deliberate actions or decision strategies that can be more community-driven) (John et al., 2020).

Secondly, the venue of action for nudges is specific and often minor in scope in terms of the modification or recalibration that they propose as a low-cost policy tool (Marteau et al., 2011; Thaler & Sunstein, 2009). The micro-perspective employed in the design of nudges, while scalable, has also attracted criticism in terms of lacking public autonomy or consent (Bovens, 2009). The procedural as well as substantive content of nudges tends to be limited to easily testable activities with randomised controlled trials (RCTs), public message framing and minor one-off changes in public actions, rather than sustained long-term behaviour change.

Thirdly, as the emphasis on a simple behavioural nudge further expands to emphasise agency, deliberation and autonomy, it goes beyond its 'one-size-fits-all' implementation and tool choices centred on information-based cues and public messaging mechanisms. A resulting, more 'think'-oriented research agenda is emerging in response, explicitly incorporating human cognition and the ability for policy targets to exercise deliberation through the design of BI operations, thus diversifying them beyond simple, micro-level readjustments or tweaks to address rationality biases (Hertwig & Grüne-Yanoff, 2017; John et al., 2020; Krueger & Funder, 2004). Recent discussions on the design of nudge 'plus' tools reflect this major development within the field (John & Stoker, 2019). While nudges are designed to work towards quick, almost automatically elicited socially desirable behaviours, the contemporary work of behavioural policy scholars indicates a consensus that some element of self-awareness, internal deliberation and participatory engagement leads to more effective implementation and long-term viability of this category of tools (Banerjee & John, 2021; Richardson & John, 2021).

In doing so, simpler assumptions about policy target decisions made inherent in nudges can be refined and augmented by making them more nudge plus, and eventually even becoming boosts, or behavioural interventions that capture more cognitive and motivational competences. For example, the framing of public announcements can help to guide policy targets to demand and accept health statistics that are based on absolute numbers (e.g. decline in the number of COVID-19 cases who are vaccinated individuals) instead of relative figures (e.g. vaccine A is x per cent more effective than vaccine B). Such efforts to 'boost' domain general competences are able to target human cognition within the environment (e.g. community norms) (Hertwig & Grüne-Yanoff, 2017; Richardson & John, 2021). Boosts are also being used to address cognitive challenges in a digital world, whereby incorrect public health information and countering fake news and disinformation have become a significant part of COVID-19 response toolkits. In other words, a successful boost relies on improving the decision-making tools available to policy targets to better deliberate and more effectively discern pertinent information (Grüne-Yanoff & Herwig, 2016).

This distinction reiterates that while nudges are used to guide target population behaviour by creating micro-level implementation conditions that trigger an action, more 'think'-oriented boosts change behaviour by cultivating more long-term and sustained competences to make better decisions. As such, there is growing agreement within the behavioural public policy community that boosting and nudging can readily complement each other by combining meso–micro-level design considerations (Richardson & John, 2021). The actual blend between them depends on the policy design goals for which they can feasibly become the means. For example, boosts are considered to be better aligned with policy designers' goals centred on producing generalised, sustained behavioural change (such as social distancing), rather than a more specific, temporary action (such as giving up a seat on a bus), wherein the latter could be simply classified as a 'nudge' (Banerjee & John, 2021; Grüne-Yanoff & Hertwig, 2016; John, 2013).

The design of 'think'-based BI means, with their more ambitious policy goal of enhanced public cognition, also encompasses a strong normative emphasis on greater public participation. Peter John and colleagues (2020), who have been at the forefront of the analysis of this category of BI devices, continuously emphasise that these tools procedurally entail more governance resources and are markedly 'harder to do' than nudges. Increased incorporation of public deliberation, autonomy and participation, which are fundamental to the design of such tools, eventually will augment the task of formulating mostly information-based interventions towards more organisation-based developments. Deliberative tools, participatory approaches and even the co-production literature that highlights broader public management implications have been empirically examined and discussed in the behavioural public policy literature as being an extension of the 'think' family of policy interventions (Durose & Richardson, 2016; John et al., 2020). The role of the state in designing these interventions is found to go beyond being the supplier of customised public information (as is the case with nudges), to becoming the creator of 'new institutional spaces to support citizen-led investigation' (John, 2013, 19), thus demanding more and different governance resources. In other words, for the 'think' design strategy, 'the policy-maker needs to be open minded and willing to act as an organizer of citizen-driven investigation' (20).

While more work is needed to conceptually better clarify the 'think' family of tools, there are broad patterns to their design that distinguish them from the more primal and simpler notion of 'nudges' (Figure 1). Firstly, despite sharing a similar starting point (in espousing notions of bounded rationality), 'thinks' propose to overcome the limits to rational behaviour through greater deliberation, more dialogue, increased participation and creation of enhanced conditions for collaboration. This agenda, which implies a significant commitment by and cost on the part of the state, is distinct in scope (more meso-level) from the design of simpler nudges that work alongside existing policies or regulations, looking to behaviourally tweak or enhance these tools at the micro-level of on-the-ground tool implementation. Secondly, as nudges go more 'along the grain' of existing tools, they supply recalibration mechanisms that are more low-cost and information-centred. By contrast, as more synergetic, cognitively sustainable behavioural outcomes are sought with the input of an increasing diversity of stakeholders, the 'think' family of behavioural tools requires more governance resources and more prominently organisational-oriented changes.

Several important next steps are needed in the policy sciences in terms of generalising about the BI family of concepts within existing efforts to classify policy instruments (Capano & Engeli, 2021). Especially pertinent are discussions about the kind of new hypotheses that need to be drawn about how BI means interact with more 'traditional' policy tools such as regulations and incentives, and especially how they interact within existing policy toolkits. The field of policy studies is at a point in theorisation that needs a focus on the outcomes of effective policies and an evaluation of the unintended consequences and side-effects of BI, which are outcome-driven. This is discussed at

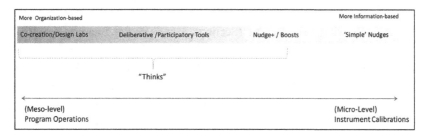

Figure 1 A continuum for BI policy design

length in Hallsworth's (2023) manifesto for applying behavioural science, in addition to several important actionable steps aimed at addressing the issues in the scope, methods and values of BI. Still, the focus of this Element is procedural rather than evaluative, so it operates on the assumption that BI instruments are adopted and implemented in a bid to increase the effectiveness of governments. In addition, some of these issues, for example policy 'over-design' (Maor, 2020), are already discussed in the policy literature.

Furthermore, what happens differently during public crisis situations? Comparative work on this question picked up in the midst of the pandemic (e.g. Bavel et al., 2020) and continues to highlight the need to address the formulation of behavioural tools in times of crisis. Hartley and Jarvis (2020), for example, in their exposition of the pandemic response in Hong Kong, call for a more nuanced exploration of how public behaviours and norm-driven motivations are constructed and proliferate during times of crisis, and what this means for community-level capacities in the face of pandemics. To tie together these important empirical insights with efforts at theorisation, this Element presents one possible 'next step' in the procedural understanding of how BI, as a policy innovation, is blended into more traditional policy design choices.

1.4 Organisation of This Element

As alluded to earlier, several important gaps are emerging in the current scholarship on BI in policy-making, which indicates the salience of the key question explored in this Element: *What are the key capacity and procedural prerequisites for the integration of BI into the design of policy tools?* The main objective of this Element is to address the pronounced lack of consolidated understanding about what is required of governments in terms of capacity and established rules of operation to effectively design behavioural insights and integrate them in multi-tool policies. This fragmentation in the literature builds on questions of whether BI tools represent a separate category or subcategory of instruments, or components of larger policy instruments (Capano & Engeli, 2021), but essentially goes further and calls for a discussion on what capabilities and procedural endowments are needed in order to integrate them into policy.

In the following two sections (Sections 2 and 3), the Element develops a discussion of a novel theoretical framework combining the academic literature on procedural policy tools and innovation adoption studies, focusing on the capacity and institutional prerequisites of BI. In Section 4, we present three illustrative case studies with respect to their experience of essential procedural endowments facilitating the effective use of BI. Namely, we introduce and discuss the broad developments in BI policy design in Australia, Singapore and the Netherlands, and their experience in creating an administrative and institutional environment conducive to effective BI utilisation. In the concluding section, we discuss the practical implications of the procedural prerequisites for BI integration in public policy-making by motivating future research questions.

2 Integrating BI into Existing Policy Toolkits: Design and Capacity Linkages

While the surge of behavioural insights penetrating the social sciences has challenged the traditional utilitarian assumptions of perfectly informed risk–benefit assessments of individuals, these assumptions still permeate much of policy design thinking with an understanding of policy target compliance (Howlett, 2018; Oliver, 2015; Thaler & Sunstein, 2009). That is, designing programmes according to the incentives and disincentives triggered by their deployment is still the main consideration occupying the majority of the literature. At the same time, the outcome of knowledge-informed policy formulation is said to result in multi-policy, multi-instrument mixes, bundles or 'packages' that may be deliberately designed to work together towards a concerted desired outcome, one that embodies a bundle of different reactions on the part of policy targets (Givoni et al., 2013).

The place of BI and behavioural public policy (BPP) within this evolving scholarship of policy design is still scattered, and yet discussions within the policy tools literature may hold the key to advancing policy design frameworks that look beyond the interaction of policy components to more deliberating espousing policy outcomes. In such policy-making scenarios, where a variety of behaviours can result from different classes of policy instruments, examining the causal inference defining how governing resources (Hood & Margetts, 2007) yield desired policy outcomes sheds more light on policy target motivations than looking at simple compliance-deterrence reactions alone. To this end, a resource-based approach as established by Christopher Hood and colleagues to instrument design choice represents one promising avenue towards unpacking the behavioural diversity that policy instruments are designed to trigger.

2.1 BI in Information and Nodality Policy Tools

Hood and Margetts (2007, 6) define this category of policy tools as pertaining to the centrality of the government in social and information networks: 'nodality equips the government with a strategic position from which to dispense information and likewise enables the government to draw in information for no other reason than that it is a centre or clearing house. The limiting factor is credibility, and the 'coin' – how government spends this resource – is messages sent and received'. Instruments in this category include government tools for information collection and release; advice and exhortation; advertising and the formation of inquiry commissions and various modes of e-government (Hood, 2007; Howlett et al., 2009). The behavioural mechanisms that are activated by this suite of instruments are grounded in information dissemination, norm-driven citizen participation and interaction, enhancing public image and knowledge sharing (Carter & Belanger, 2005; Dawes, 1996) and increasing public accountability for social behaviours (Andersen & Dawes, 1991; Gil-Garcia & Martinez-Moyano, 2007).

Nodality-based instruments can also work to establish and ingrain prevailing norms and ideas about appropriate interactions, participation and coordination. That is, the norm-informed trajectory of such policy instruments can precede self-maximising calculations on the part of policy targets, and also reflect the dominance of a particular intervention logic that directs and constrains policy choice (Bernstein, 2001; Bernstein & Cashore, 2012; Cashore et al., 2019). Furthermore, with the advent of information technology and unprecedented technical advancements, such tools of 'nodality', or those that depend on the government to communicate with policy targets, collect and disseminate information, establish cognitive frames of appropriateness, sway civic actions or persuade members of society to comply with public directives, can be seen to be increasingly crucial to the success of all other categories of policy tools.

Furthermore, the evolution of networks of information sharing has brought information as a policy resource to many actors beyond governments. This scenario is in contrast to Hood's original, earlier conceptualisation of this class of instruments, whereby nodality was considered to be an endowment that the government possesses 'by virtue of being government' (Hood, 2007). This is because, from a mechanistic perspective, information tools are better adapted to activate 'first-order' behaviours such as citizen engagement and interaction and information diffusion, while for second-order behaviours and cognitive commitments made through public participation in policy, nodality appears to activate coordination as well as the redistribution of power.

2.2 BI in Authority-Based and Regulatory Policy Tools

Instruments of regulation mainly exercise government control and authority, and they therefore closely reflect the use of mechanisms related to coercion. Popular styles of regulation-based policy instruments include command-and-control systems, laws and mandates, and forms of delegated and (self-)regulation

(Salamon, 2000). Most types of regulation and authority instruments award 'the legitimate legal or official power to command or prohibit' societal actions to the government (Margetts & Hood, 2016). Economic regulations, such as those governing the prices and volumes of agricultural resources or regulating pollution and other environmental offences, are formulated to control particular aspects of a market economy (including the entry or exit of firms), influence the return on investments and correct perceived inequities in economic relationships (Salamon, 2000). The progression of such tools strongly reflects the 'rules' pathway identified by Bernstein and Cashore (2000, 2012). Bernstein and Cashore (2000) use the example of regulatory mandates and agreements, which demand a focus on not just how and how well rules and regulations are followed but also the influence of such rules on problem definitions and recasting of policy goals in line with policy target compliance. As discussed previously, behavioural mechanisms activated based on the government's exercise of coercive powers and regulatory alignment lead to second-tier mechanisms related to monitoring compliance, political legitimation, blame-avoidance and isomorphic dynamics. One example of the importance of BI for regulatory action is the multiple regulations set up by the European Commission, such as data protection, regulation of privacy, consumer protection and business conduct, among others (see Alemanno & Sibony, 2015).

In the case of self-regulation or voluntary agreements, sometimes also known as 'non-state market driven' (NSMD) governance, a different set of behavioural mechanisms can encourage voluntary certification schemes whereby industry conglomerations develop and certify standards of good business practice (such as the sustainability certification of ecologically detrimental agricultural products and practices) (Auld et al., 2009). This class of instruments usually activates behavioural mechanisms such as compliance, normative isomorphism and participation. The second set of such mechanisms set off by these practices concerns building legitimacy and gaining political acceptance as an authority-based instrument. These mechanisms are required because the success of modes of self-regulation is heavily dependent on how effectively they are able to develop contextually grounded institutions and endure as politically feasible rule-making entities (Ostrom, 2000). Often, these legitimacy-seeking mechanisms also depend on how well self-regulation systems 'create and maintain appropriate structures of property rights, rule governing contracts, liability rules' (Brondizio et al., 2009, 39).

2.3 BI in Treasure-Based or Financial Policy Tools

The functioning of this class of policy instruments relies heavily on the allocation of public wealth and financial resources, as well as on the ways in which the

government raises and distributes funds. Mechanisms based on utility calculations and the weighing of incentives versus disincentives are most closely
linked with this family of policy instruments. The deployment of incentives
or disincentives can unleash causal processes or behavioural responses akin to
those identified in the 'markets' pathway by Bernstein and Cashore (2000,
2012). The use of such instruments encompasses the entire gamut of financial
tools at the disposal of the government, such as subsidies in the form of grants,
tax incentives and loans (to reinforce desirable economic activities), as well as
taxes and user charges (to raise government funds or penalise socially undesir-
able behaviour) (Howlett et al., 2009). Government expenditures of the former
sort, especially grants, are offered to support 'some end worthy in itself,
sometimes as a form of recognition, reward or encouragement' (Pal, 1992,
152). Tax incentives or the reduction or deferral of payments owed to the
state are another form of subsidy (Mitnick, 1980). Subsidies as a class of
instruments make specific use of incentivising as the main mechanism of their
deployment.

By contrast, taxes and user charges provide financial deterrents to curb some
aspect of society or modify the consumption behaviour of an economy. Taxes
can be deployed for a wide array of public goals, and as such, the primary
behavioural mechanisms that are activated by taxes are disincentives because
they increase the cost of a particular action or behaviour, especially the consumption (e.g. sugar tax) or production patterns of private market goods.
Support for innovation as a mechanism may follow to uphold the efficient
production of such goods and services. Similarly, when taxes are employed to
compensate for public ills, such as environmental taxes to curb carbon emissions, they may be followed by innovation in pursuit of more efficient practices
and competition among existing industry players. From the perspective of
norms, through the use of such taxes, governments are able to activate
a reorientation of public values and linked priorities between broad goals such
as environmental protection and economic development.

2.4 Organisation-Based Governance Resources for BI Design: A Research Gap?

The research agenda of behavioural public policy (BPP) and behavioural public
administration (BPA) has also tended to focus on more micro-level individual
behavioural processes, with comparatively less attention to broader political,
social and, at the policy level, organisational considerations of the procedural
aspects of BI design (Ewert et al., 2021; Moynihan, 2018). As a result,
a prevailing criticism faced by the BI policy scholarship is that most analytical

approaches to studying BI in the policy process remain descriptive with a limited scope when it comes to accommodating different policy-making contexts as well as discussing how the instrumental, organisational and macro-political considerations of behavioural policy formulation are related to each other, even when taking a comparative view (Battaglio et al., 2019; Feitsma & Whitehead, 2022). In response to these observations, recent discourse on the 'what next' of BI policy studies has highlighted that in investigating the organisational implications of BI policy, 'they should produce concrete practical insights for the management and performance of and decision-making in public organizations, the success and failure of network collaboration and contribute to the diagnosis, evaluation and development of policy design and its assumptions' (Ewert et al., 2021, 5).

In other words, while the literature remains steadfastly focused on the public outcomes and effects of BPP, scholars have cautioned that in perceiving nudges and minor behavioural calibrations as more 'simple' than traditional policy instruments, their organisational design and administration may also be misconstrued as being simple. Relevant experience from the environmental sector, for example, indicates that while nudges have been reportedly treated as 'easy' and comparatively 'low-cost', their design has necessitated extensive research on human behaviour, in particular multilevel contexts such as sustainability (Mont et al., 2014). That significant effort to generate and allocate resources, capabilities and knowledge is often needed to access, review and incorporate this research from behavioural economics and psychology into nudge policy design may not be fully reflected in studies surrounding their implementation. Further, integrating this evidence in different policy domains (such as health, environment and public spending) is often a separate endeavour from using it for adjusting existing policy instruments (such as regulations versus tax incentives) (Giest & Mukherjee, 2018).

Additionally, the vast diversity of behavioural interventions, as indicated in Section 1, has warranted a proliferation of methodological innovations that help policy-makers go beyond just looking at behaviours that defy economic rationality. Modern behavioural public policy is developing as a multidisciplinary and multi-methodological concept that derives insights from 'anthropology, geography and sociology as well as the application of qualitative methods' (Ewert & Loer, 2021, 25). This awareness further suggests that while certain methods (such as experimental social science research, and most prominently RCTs) have dominated the behavioural policy formulation arena, it is likely not to remain limited to these approaches as the field advances. For example, research on incorporating behavioural insights into policy design burgeoned in response to COVID-19 as governments sought to improve the outcomes of regulatory-based tools (lockdown-related prohibitions), safe-distancing measures and curbing the spread of disinformation, to name a few (Debnath & Bardhan, 2020). The application of RCTs in refining BI design, in this situation, necessitated mobilisation beyond labs and government research units to quickly translate 'improved' designs into practice, thereby heavily relying on methods such as qualitative research, participatory action research and network analysis to inform policy design (Abaluck et al., 2022; van Roekel et al., 2023).

Focusing on these developments, this section organises what is known about government's institutional and organisational considerations for behavioural public policy by outlining the procedural resources and instruments, policy capacities and subject expertise necessary for their effective design as public policy.

This discussion is keenly aware of other factors that play a role in BI adoption and implementation, such as the role of epistemic communities (Simons and Schniedermann 2021; Weible 2018), transnational knowledge brokers (Feitsma, 2019) and the shift towards RCT in policy, and in evaluation of BI tools specifically (Banerjee et al., 2020; de Souza Leão & Eyal, 2019). There is an acknowledgement of the extent to which policy translation played a role in BI adoption in the cases used in this Element. However, the primary scope of this Element is firmly on addressing the gap of the organisational aspects of adoption and implementation of BI at the national level. The research gap in the interplay between national-level organisational resources and transnational communities is important and should be addressed in future research.

2.5 Procedural Resources and Instruments

Unlike substantive instruments, which have frequently been the topic of analysis in the policy sciences, procedural instruments have enjoyed much less academic investigation, and this is also starkly evident in the study of behavioural policy. Procedural instruments are understood as those resources and actions that go towards supporting the administrative and managerial processes taking place within government for the design of policy. As such, their study reflects the scholarly overlap between public administration and the policy sciences and includes an exploration of government's own instruments, created to support its internal design and policy formulation activities. These instruments include network management mechanisms and public participation, activities linked to the delivery of organisational services, such as the formation of advisory committees to regulatory agencies, and policy processes more generally, such as the creation of public information commissions, government data portals and repositories and judicial review processes (Howlett, 2018). Such instruments are designed internally within the government to support the creation of substantive policy instruments – such as taxes, subsidies or public awareness campaigns – that directly impact public and societal behaviour.

Unlike substantive tools that directly affect the production, consumption and distribution activities of public goods and services, procedural instruments have been envisioned as instead focusing on affecting governments' own internal actions related to the policy-making process. For example, network management and governing the behaviours and interactions of policy-making agents is one significant function of procedural tools (Klijn et al., 1995). Beyond their administrative function, procedural elements can also shape the substantive policy decisions that follow from government's process-oriented actions. Examples include government forming an advisory committee of select citizens or experts to help timely deliberations on sensitive issues such as nuclear energy regulation, or the creation of freedom-of-information or access-to-information laws facilitating citizen access to government legislation and records. Additionally, reorganising an administration's own internal structure can impact the effective formulation of policies, as occurs when new regulating agencies are created by merging personnel from energy and environmental ministries, forcing the two to adopt a new collaborative operating arrangement.

Organisational changes made to initially set up or further broaden BI-centred policy design within government may be as radical or distinct as setting up of a new nudge unit or appointing new personnel, or more incremental as the commissioning of one-off pilots or experiments within existing policy initiatives. In the first instance, the popularity of nudges and other behavioural interventions have been seen to propagate the creation of specialised policy advisory bodies or behavioural insight units to consolidate expertise on public behaviour and citizen choice (Halpern, 2015b). Often referred to as behavioural insights teams (BITs), per their origins in the United Kingdom and the United States, these units have emerged as the main originators of policy formulation activities explicitly based on understanding the 'choice architectures' of public policy targets. As expressed by Thaler and Sunstein (2009), such experts take on the role of 'choice architects' who have 'the responsibility for organizing the context in which people make decisions ... there is no such thing as a "neutral" design' (1). As such, in contemporary policy formulation situations, BITs have thus been instrumental as activators of policy designs that are specifically aimed at bringing about modest yet measurable modifications in the actions of the public towards socially and environmentally desirable behaviours through the use of 'nudges' and other behavioural cues. Often supplementing the use of traditional instruments that make use of government resources of coercion, law enforcement or fiscal endowments, BITs are tasked with designing mechanisms able to stimulate nearly subconscious compliance with government directives

(Howlett, 2018). For example, BITs have been widely successful in helping to reduce energy consumption by working with public utilities to display own and peer electricity-use patterns for households (Lehner et al., 2016; Rafiq et al., 2016).

In other situations, whereby the diffusion of behavioural insights research and policy design has been more variable, behavioural experts or consultants may negotiate institutional logics within the government in a more incremental fashion, especially in 'backstage' governance contexts that have previously rejected strong rationalist ideas prior to engaging with BI (Feitsma, 2018). For example, Feitsma's (2018) critical ethnography of behavioural experts at work for policy-making (in the example of the Netherlands, which is covered in this Element) has depicted four main 'balancing acts' on the part of experts that have organisational bases, namely, 'knowledge brokering, focusing on outputs, analytical satisficing and horizontalizing the hierarchy of evidence' (160), which determine the negotiation of the institutional logics of their work within the government. Analytical capacities and expertise are further discussed in the remainder of this section.

2.5.1 Capacities

The analytical capabilities and skills needed for BI policy design can traverse substantive as well as procedural aspects of policy formulation (Mukherjee et al., 2021; Wu et al., 2015). Policy design commits policy-making to deliberately and systematically endeavouring to analyse how targets react or change their behaviours in response to instruments of governance (Peters et al., 2018). Effective design subsequently involves applying the knowledge gained about instrument–target relationships to the creation of policies that can then predictably lead to desired policy outcomes (Bobrow & Dryzek, 1987; Gilabert & Lawford-Smith, 2012; Peters et al., 2018; Sidney, 2007). These activities are based on the assumption that feasible polices can be realistically generated through effective design processes only when, firstly, contradictions internal to the substantive content of policy are resolved or minimised and, secondly, when the necessary capacities and capabilities to enact design procedures are in place (Bali et al., 2021; Mukherjee & Bali, 2019).

The discussion of analytical capacities for behavioural public administration often converges on the centrality of experimental research methods and randomised controlled trials (RCTs) (Van Ryzin 2021). As Oliver (2015) summarises in their overview of the study of behavioural public administration, 'behavioural public policy is the application of insights from behavioural economics specifically and behavioural science more broadly to public policy design', indicating a strong link between the analysis of behavioural science theory and its application through an intervention. In actuality, and as Van Ryzin (2021) and Feitsma (2018, 2019) have observed, the process of trial and error and the actual practice of designing behavioural interventions is deliberately incremental, whereby there is a great deal of 'learning by failure' alongside 'learning by doing'.

The notable behavioural 'turn' in public policy is often sketched alongside the parallel development of behavioural economics. Behavioural public policy scholars often and strongly allude to the steady institutionalisation and professionalisation of behavioural economics through its application in the public sector and the concurrent rise in the use of experimental methods for evidence-based policy-making (Strassheim & Beck, 2019; Datta & Mullainathan, 2014). However, this observation of the growing presence of experimental methods for the practice-oriented development of behavioural insights for policy does not yet present generalisable findings about related analytical, organisational and political capacities that are needed through the process of institutionalisation within the government. Nor does it allude to how these capacities interact with and potentially fluctuate for policy formulation, beyond evaluation.

Recent bibliometric analyses of the maturation of methodological capacities linked with behavioural public policy design suggest significant geographic variability, with behavioural studies concentrated in the United States until the 2000s, with European and developed Asian nations following through the decade post-2010 (Rawat, 2019). Studies from developing nations or regions such as Africa and South America are scant in comparison, with the most prominent studies linked to the work of organisations specialising in the application of RCT methodologies, or financial organisations working towards poverty alleviation in the development sector, often with significant institutional challenges to scaling up behavioural research beyond programmes and towards policy. As exemplified in Box 1, this is particularly the case in developing countries wherein the greatest limiting factor inhibiting the effective design of programmes may be to do with scaling up evidence derived from research experiments.

Trial-and-error approaches and experimentation in real-world situations are generally understood as the main analytical capacities linked to the design of behavioural instruments (Thierer, 2016). Since most behavioural interventions and mechanisms are developing beyond their infancy, according to Abdukadirov (2016), 'nudge designers must rely on a trial-and-error process to weed out bad ideas and refine promising nudges' (5). Government can then decide how to adjust certain policy instruments to create the desired behaviour based on these findings. However, due to policy-making being informed by the

Box 1 Designing behavioural programmes in multilateral
development banks (MDBs)

A link between poverty and behaviour has long been alluded to in the work
of MDBs in Asia. The explicit articulation of this connection, however,
has only been made over the last five years as behavioural insights have
been deliberately designed into poverty alleviation programmes. Directly
linked to the earlier discussion of the behavioural implications of three
major policy instrument classifications is the growing claim from development practitioners that behavioural research can 'make development
policies more effective. Standard development policy typically targets
financial resources, laws or incentives' (World Bank, 2014). The World
Bank is currently the forerunner among MDBs in Asia to design behavioural interventions into their development projects. In their 2015 World
Development Report (WDR), the World Bank explicitly stated that 'poverty is not simply a shortfall of money. The constant day-to-day hard
choices with poverty in effect "tax" an individual's psychological and
social resources (80). This type of "tax" can lead to economic decisions
that perpetuate poverty' (World Bank, 2015, 80). Emphasising the psychological dimension of poverty alleviation, the creation of a dedicated
unit of behavioural experts within the World Bank has, for instance,
enhanced the institutionalisation of the design of behavioural interventions within development programmes financed by multilateral development institutions or MDIs (World Bank, 2015). For the Asian
Development Bank, communicating behavioural change represents
a crucial part of its due diligence as it allows projects to 'get off on the
right foot by considering user behaviour and actual needs. Key stakeholders are engaged because they know more about what they need and,
when involved, can provide innovative and pragmatic solutions' (Asian
Development Bank, 2017). This sentiment arises from a growing realisation in development work that casting project objectives from the perspective of behavioural change sustains positive outcomes after and well
beyond when a programme is deemed to have been completed.
Reframing urban and rural sanitation as a behaviour change rather than
as a finite output of a development programme, for example, has consistently been shown to improve the effectiveness and sustainability of
desired outcomes (Mukherjee & Mukherjee, 2018).

Further yet, the use of behavioural insights towards development programmes and projects is being viewed as a way of explicitly contextualis-
ing design and customising an intervention based on local, social and

psychological influences. Especially given that one of the main mechanisms employed by behavioural insights is the use of social norms to alter target behaviour, they have been included in policy programmes as a way to achieve better alignment with local contexts. Examples include using existing local social networks as a way of transferring information, instead of creating a more formal mode of communication with programme participants of conditional cash transfer (CCT) programmes; and speeding up the adoption of crop insurance or microcredit loans by engaging the participation of community leaders, who then in turn encourage more wider adoption or buy-in. These choices have led to more lasting outcomes post-implementation as they have focused on the outset on mobilising communities to change social norms.

precautionary principle, some governments have refrained from using this information in the first place because of the risks involved in scaling up the 'learning-by-doing' approach to behavioural insights. The interdependence of policy instruments is also ambiguous as a result of learning-by-doing because policies may have intended and unforeseen consequences that are not always documented (Nauwelaers & Wintjes 2008); one example is using monetary incentives to nudge people into donating blood, resulting in the crowding out of donation behaviours by women in Sweden (Mellström & Johannesson, 2008). The context specificity of trial runs also makes the transfer of those findings to other policy domains less probable. Administrative costs related to information processing and coordination can stymie managerial capabilities by rising in a non-linear fashion (Mani, 2021). Mani (2021) goes on to describe this unequal transition as causing a 'voltage drop' between the design of tools through field experiments and their subsequent contribution to the design of programmes (103).

Currently available behavioural intervention research involving experimental methods also deals with issues related to sample size versus sample type and capabilities related to translating results into policy-relevant findings. That is, results of experimental methods in the behavioural public policy space frequently depend on studying populations whose size, as opposed to quality, is a criterion. Among other criticisms levelled at RCTs that warrant caution in their application are the limited ability of RCTs to deal with complexity, as they require stable and simple contexts (Hallsworth, 2023), and the lack of external validity in its traditional sense due to extremely limited samples (Deaton & Cartwright, 2018). Furthermore, the government may be interested in specific interventions for subpopulations (such as the elderly, single parents or children in primary school), even if large, more heterogenous samples would be important for generalising the results of behavioural studies. Therefore, in order to understand 'how cultural preferences, attitudes, and economic outcomes may differently affect segments of the population such as low-income groups', larger, more granular statistics are needed for policy design, but they may be seldom available (Maddix, 2017, 1).

At the outset, the entirety of analytical capacities dealing with experimental methods, RCTs and testing interventions to derive and deliver relevant lessons for policy formulation may be embodied in specialised contracted consultants or dedicated BITs. However, these cannot be readily substituted for the more organisational capabilities of translating behavioural policy advice, or for political capacities related to fostering collaboration, socialisation and garnering of stakeholder support for behavioural policy interventions more broadly. In their exposition of BITs in Australia, for example, Ball and Head (2021) surmise that 'the scientific nature of RCTs is supposed to "depoliticise" the evaluation of policy options; however, this masks the political nature of selecting research questions and instruments, as well as the substantive exclusion of the voices of users and citizens' (120). The design of behavioural interventions, therefore, is viewed as much more than the craft necessary to design 'just another policy tool' (Ewert, 2020).

2.5.2 Expertise and Policy Change

Lastly, accompanying the organisational and capacity considerations that can define the procedural side of behavioural policy design is the discussion of knowledge agents and expertise. As discussed previously, in the constellation of political actors who are involved in the process of policy formulating, BITs have been notably shown occupy a unique position of being subject-matter experts who contribute to the knowledge and information used in policy-making. Owing to their specialised expertise, BITs also perform the role of design decision makers with significant say in the structure and content of instruments based on behavioural insights.

A number of governments have formed so-called nudge units to support the behavioural aspects of their policy-making efforts, often drawing inspiration from the original British experience with BITs. These teams of behavioural science experts are tasked with 'designing behavioral interventions that have the potential to encourage desirable behavior without restricting choice, testing those interventions rapidly and inexpensively, and then widely implementing the strategies that prove most effective' (Benartzi et al., 2017, 10). However, there is often limited thought given to the nature of knowledge or the data dimension of these studies. In other words, governments often lack the expertise to match the data generated for and by behavioural research, to draw on a broader foundation that is commensurate with the design of behavioural components and those of existing, more traditional measures. In a report on BIs, the OECD (2017a), for example, specifically outlines the importance of data by saying that 'good and reliable data is . . . required if behavioral insights are to become robust policy tools' (OECD 2017a, 4). This lack of expertise also leads to what the OECD (2017a) calls an 'implementation gap' where behavioural insights are largely used for fine-tuning at a late stage of policy-making when instruments are already in place rather than facilitating the effectiveness of policy and regulation before designing the instrument.

Finally, there are two additional aspects about expertise that bear mention for making the connection between the design of behavioural policy tools and larger policy change. Firstly, there are limited efforts in policy circles to assess the cost effectiveness of these types of instruments and interventions may actually be quite minimal adjustments to policy settings Van Ryzin (2021). This makes it difficult to estimate whether a tool 'increases engagement in a desired behavior by a larger amount per dollar spent than a traditional intervention' (Benartzi et al. 2017, 10). And, secondly, small experiments with limited generalisation ability can rarely serve as a justification to expand behavioural instruments in other policy areas. Results so far show that the outcomes of tangible policy change in OECD countries are mixed (OECD 2017a) despite the prevalence and growing presence of behavioural expertise. Countries that have been dealing with behavioural insights for a longer period of time have largely focused on changes 'mostly on improving implementation (e.g. letter to tax payers, access to information, default options, etc.) . . . there was hardly any information in the survey about examples where insights-related initiatives had been transferred to policy thinking generally, and whether there had been an evaluation of its success' (OECD 2017, 44).

Some concrete examples of policy change that are more at the programme level do exist; however, these have remained one-off examples without much scope for generalising beyond specific contexts (Rangone, 2018, Lodge & Wegrich, 2016). Findings from the transport sector, for example, where experiments in retail settings were conducted with regard to the labelling of car fuel efficiency, showed that 'translating fuel efficiency indicators into expected fuel costs throughout a period of multiple years can be highly effective in driving consumers towards the purchase of more fuel efficient vehicles' (EPOC, 2017, 31). The applications of behavioural insights around simplifying and framing information, in order to increase the effectiveness of fuel efficiency labels and their role in car choice, led the United States Environmental Protection Agency (US-EPA) to mandate a change in the framing of fuel efficiency labels in 2011 to include information on the fuel costs associated with car use (EPOC, 2017). Additional (linked) data can support these efforts by providing potential insights beyond specific policy sectors and further compare different mixes of policy instruments and their effectiveness.

2.6 What Next?

How, then, can we explore the ways in which experience with behavioural public policy as an innovation is changing and in turn being changed by governments' own work? The general discourse strongly indicates that the use of BI in policy represents a coming-of-age example of policy innovation and is more than just a passing policy fad (Battaglio Jr. et al., 2019; Straßheim, 2020), especially considering the rise of artificial intelligence (AI) and its potential to augment behavioural science to develop targeted nudges based on large swaths of data. The rise of the digital BI tools, G2C (government-to-citizen) governance, regulation of the web and so forth make this discussion even more timely and pertinent. While it is still not clear to what extent BI will penetrate policy-making and existing frameworks of policy instrument choice in the long term, or whether it will even eventually be recognised as a policy tool on its own rather than an extension of the existing instruments (Hill & Varone, 2016; Kosters & Van der Heijden, 2015), BI remains at the foreseeable forefront of policy design ambitions in many countries around the world (Afif et al., 2019).

With this in mind, there are still important, yet presently unanswered questions to be asked about the necessary procedural and administrative endowments of governments for the successful and appropriate integration of BI, as a policy innovation, into the existing policy design framework. Behavioural insight's institutionalisation as a governance innovation is discussed in the following section.

3 Institutionalisation of BI through Innovation Adoption

The use of BI in policy is a relatively recent phenomenon that, until just under two decades ago, was an approach rarely taken in policy-making. The intellectual and scientific underpinnings of BI can be traced back to the behavioural turn in applied social sciences in the 1960s and 1970s, with government forays into understanding the impact of individual behaviours and preferences becoming more prominent in the 1970s and 1980s, particularly as part of evaluating major social welfare programmes, such as education, benefits and public health (Jones et al., 2021). Still, in its current form BI made its way into policy-making as a result of the confluence of several important factors, such as the rise of evidence-based policy, preference for deregulation and increasing cooperation between behavioural economists and psychology experts, which, coupled with the fiscal pressures of the global financial crisis and the publication of Thaler and Sunstein's (2009) seminal text, served as a catalyst for promoting the use of BI in government (Jones et al., 2013). BI was seen as a low-cost innovation that could improve programme outcomes (Jones et al., 2020). We are especially interested in this approach to BI as essentially a policy innovation.

With this in mind, we adopt a perspective on procedural policy design whereby we highlight the policy capacities required at different stages of innovation (Damanpour & Schneider, 2006; Howlett, 2000; Howlett & Ramesh, 2016; Roberts, 1988; Wu et al., 2015). The innovation adoption literature is particularly pertinent for analysing the institutionalisation of new categories of tools such as BI (Ball & Head, 2021; Einfeld & Blomkamp, 2021; John, 2018). These new tools of government offer innovative ways to tackle wicked problems through experimentation but often come without the requisite perspective on the best ways to implement them and ensure their sustainability. This is where the innovation perspective of BI may be helpful for unpacking how BI may be institutionalised in policy-making. The three stages of innovation adoption that are critical for understanding the institutionalisation of BI tools in existing regulatory frameworks are loosely based on the seminal work by Roberts (1988) and commonly include initiation, decision adoption and implementation (Damanpour & Schneider, 2006; Klein & Sorra, 1996; Pichlak, 2016; Walker et al., 2001; Zaltman et al., 1973). In adopting this perspective, our goal is to devise an analytical starting point for comparatively examining the institutionalisation of BI tool formulation processes within governments.

Much has been said regarding the factors that affect innovation adoption, at every stage. There are also various perspectives on managing innovation in organisations, pioneered by Roberts (1988), who provided a detailed overview of the main organisational factors that facilitate innovation adoption success. Our aim is to bring into focus these various perspectives on managing innovation in organisations by zooming in specifically on one type of innovation – BI – in a very specific type of context – government.

3.1 Stages of Innovation Adoption

The existing frameworks of the innovation adoption process vary from the two-stage (Gopalkrishnan & Damanpour, 1997) to more detailed models that cover three (Damanpour et al., 2009; Hameed et al., 2012), five (Klein & Sorra, 1996), six (Frambach & Schillewaert, 2002) or more stages (Kwon & Zmud, 1987).

Some authors conceptualised this process as linear (Howieson et al., 2014), while others argued for a dynamic and recursive approach characterised by feedback and feed-forward loops (Adams et al., 2006). However, the most frequently used approach to the innovation adoption process is the 'unitary sequence model', divided into three more general phases: initiation, adoption decision and implementation, consistent with Lewin's (1952) model of the change process. In this section, we rely on this conceptualisation of the innovation adoption process and describe these three stages in more detail.

3.1.1 Initiation

This stage, which can be also known as pre-adoption, refers to a number of activities that reflect the search for solutions as a response to recognising a need for such solutions (Damanpour & Schneider, 2006). It involves acquiring knowledge or awareness of existing innovation, forming an initial attitude towards it and proposing innovation for adoption (Hameed et al., 2012; Rogers, 1995). It encompasses awareness, consideration and intention substages (Frambach & Schillewaert, 2002).

For example, the work carried out by the UK Nudge Unit on increasing the rate of tax revenue collection was preceded by an intensive search for possible solutions to the existing problem of insufficient tax compliance. A particular focus on high transaction activities, such as revenue collection, is related to the relative ease with which randomisation can occur, the statistical power of interventions with a large sample size and clear financial benefits to the agency from the high volume of payments, as even small percentage changes in outcomes can significantly affect revenue flows. With this in mind, the Nudge Unit explored a number of options that included simplification of messages and social norms. The former was aimed at reducing the cognitive burden of reading the message, while the latter utilised the individual propensity to conform and succumb to social pressure (John & Blume, 2018). The research and experimentation conducted based on these two assumptions informed subsequent propositions for the design of the message on a tax bill.

3.1.2 Decision Adoption

The adoption decision stage involves the decision to accept the proposed idea by evaluating the desired solution from practical, strategic, financial and/or technological perspectives (Damanpour & Schneider, 2006) and allocating resources for its acquisition (Hameed et al., 2012). In this stage, top managers expand perceptions of an innovation to decide whether it will support the development of organisational goals and objectives (Kirkman, 2012).

At this stage, organisations and governments often seek additional evidence that innovation really works. For example, a decision to adopt innovation may be preceded by commissioning research studies and trials that would demonstrate the value added, as was the case in Australia. Research work was commissioned by the National Preventative Health Taskforce in 2008–2009 on measures to encourage better choices concerning nutrition, exercise, smoking and alcohol reduction (Moodie, 2008); and additional research was commissioned on how better urban planning could encourage 'active' forms of recreation and journey-to-work (Garrard et al., 2008), before any decisions were made to adopt innovative BI solutions.

3.1.3 Implementation

The implementation (postadoption) stage deals with activities related to modifying the innovation, preparing the organisation for its general use (Damanpour & Schneider, 2006), performing a trial for its confirmation and providing the acceptance of an innovation by an organisation and its employees (Hameed et al., 2012; Rogers, 1995).

An example of decision adoption to use BI is the United States in 2015, when the US president signed an executive order establishing the practice of using behavioural science in federal government agencies by applying behavioural insights in policies and programmes. The same order created the Social and Behavioural Science Team under the National Science and Technology Council. The executive order signifies that resources have been allocated for the innovation; its use was not just accepted but mandated, and its overall benefit confirmed.

3.2 Determinants of Innovation Adoption

Beyond exploring what stages comprise the innovation adoption process, scholarly attention has been paid to factors that contribute to innovation adoption. Since our primary interest lies in the institutionalisation of BI, we are particularly keen on understanding what organisational antecedents serve as an important impetus for innovation adoption. This is crucial for the theoretical development of the requisite institutional arrangements for effective BI utilisation in government policy. One of the efforts that discusses organisational and top management characteristics that aid innovation adoption can be seen in Pichlak (2015), which proposes two factors: organisational structure and resources.

In this section, we discuss how neatly institutionalisation of BI in terms of procedural instruments, three types of capacities – analytical, political, and managerial – and knowledge and expertise can be fitted into the framework of innovation adoption determinants at every stage of adoption. Pichlak's (2015) effort, used here as a guiding framework, provides a useful heuristic as to what is required at every innovation adoption stage for the innovation to succeed. We attempt to synthesise insights from the innovation adoption literature with those from the public policy and public administration literature in order to produce a theoretical approach, which we further develop throughout the remainder of this Element.

3.2.1 Organisational Structure

Organisational structure is often seen as one of the most crucial determinants of innovation adoption. Pichlak (2015) argues in favour of understanding individual attributes of the organisational structure and structural antecedents of innovation adoption such as: specialisation, horizontal and vertical differentiation, centralisation, formalisation and professionalism (Baldridge & Burnham, 1975; Damanpour, 1991; Damanpour & Schneider, 2006; Kimberly & Evanisko, 1981; Pierce & Delbecq, 1977). She relates these structural variables to different phases of the innovation adoption process in order to address how an organisation's structural characteristics affect innovation adoption.

Specialisation represents the number of different specialties found in an organisation (Damanpour, 1991; Kimberly & Evanisko, 1981). Horizontal differentiation (also known as functional or structural differentiation) represents the extent to which an organisation is divided into a number of smaller units (Damanpour, 1991; Kimberly & Evanisko, 1981). Vertical differentiation refers to the number of levels in an organisation's hierarchy (Damanpour, 1991). Centralisation describes the locus of authority and decision-making in the organisation. This is also indicative of the distribution of decision-making autonomy – or its concentration (Damanpour, 1991). Finally, formalisation points to the extent to which rules and procedures are defined, adhered to and enforced, as well as the level of their flexibility (Damanpour, 1991).

The impact of the organisational structure by phase of the innovation adoption process is not something that has been explored extensively in the innovation literature. This is a regrettable oversight, because, just as the nature of organisations is dynamic, so must be the impact of the organisational structures on the process of innovation adoption. The novelty of Pichlak's (2015) approach is her attempt to reconcile the two by conducting a Delphi-method study with 264 experts on innovation adoption.

The experts expressed the view that specialisation and horizontal differentiation as two indicators of organisational complexity are significant, crucial factors at the initiation stage. This echoes the finding by Damanpour and Schneider (2006) that organisational complexity has a positive effect on initiation but not on adoption decision and implementation. This is due to the increased possibility of cross-fertilisation of ideas (Pierce & Delbecq, 1977), depth and diversity of knowledge (Damanpour et al., 2009), which are more likely to manifest in complex organisations and thus spur creativity, increase awareness of new solutions and encourage innovative suggestions. Organisational complexity is correlated with better access to information and knowledge about various innovations and a higher likelihood to identify those (Damanpour & Schneider, 2006).

Centralisation is typically associated with efficiency in decision processes (Prajogo & McDermott, 2014); however it may negatively affect the second and the third stages of innovation adoption in a number of ways. Firstly, it reduces the involvement and commitment of organisational members due to narrowing the locus of authority and decision-making rights among the organisational members (Aiken & Hage, 1971; Pierce & Delbecq, 1977). Secondly, it may limit the free flow of ideas (Prajogo & McDermott, 2014) and therefore hinder the development of more innovative solutions (Atuahene-Gima, 2003). At the other end of the spectrum is the flexibility in decision-making, which encourages the adoption of innovation by involving the organic formation of social networks and making more information available to them (Damanpour & Schneider, 2006; Lewis & Seibold, 1993).

Formalisation, as expressed in rigid rules and job descriptions within an organisation, acts as a strong inhibitor of the implementation stage. This is due to the role played by formalisation in the acceptance of an innovation by an organisation and its employees. Formalisation affects postadoption activities and authority relationships, for example the creation of standardised activities and systems, and encourages employees to incorporate these into existing routines (Prajogo & McDermott, 2014).

This is echoed by Frambach and Schillewaert (2002), who argue that organisational, or adopter, characteristics are crucial determinants of innovation adoption. These include size, structure and organisational innovativeness. For example, size is found to be positively correlated with innovation adoption as bigger organisations tend to have the need to adopt innovations. Organisation structure has been found to either enable or inhibit innovation adoption. Formalisation and centralisation, as structural characteristics of organisations, may be instrumental for innovation implementation but may create challenges at the initiation level (Zaltman et al., 1973). The opposite holds for organisations that are highly complex or specialised. Unlike Pichlak (2015), Frambach and Schillewaert (2002) do not offer any thoughts on which adopter characteristics are crucial at which stage of innovation adoption.

We argue that what Pichlak (2015) is describing as an organisational prerequisite for innovation adoption in terms of organisational structure is essentially one type of a procedural policy tool. Organisational structure indirectly defines and constrains organisational decisions and affects the process of innovation adoption in the same way procedural tools indirectly affect and shape policy formulation and implementation (Bali et al., 2021). Governments rely on a range of procedural tools, defined by Bali et al. (2021) as 'administrative processes and activities for selecting, deploying, and calibrating' (298) new policies and ideas (Howlett & Ramesh, 1998). Therefore, we propose that having procedural tools in place, including a conducive organisational structure, is the first precondition for innovation adoption. However, building on the innovation adoption literature and incorporating insights from public policy and administration scholarship, we expand the set of essential procedural tools for BI design and implementation beyond organisational structure and characteristics, as discussed later in this section.

3.2.2 Resources

Innovation adoption relies on the availability of resources, according to the resource-based view of the company (Barney, 1991). An organisation's resources can be divided into two categories – financial resources and human resources – that contribute to its competitive advantage (Adams et al., 2006; Ahuja et al., 2008).

Human resources refers to skilled, qualified employees who possess expertise in specific domains and thus contribute to creativity (Karaman Akgul & Gozlu, 2015; Helfat & Martin, 2015). Employees' tacit knowledge creates complementarity, which in turn increases the positive consequences of the adoption of innovation in organisations. Financial resources enable innovation by neutralising a risk (Barney, 1991), absorbing the cost of failure (Damanpour et al., 2009), widening the possibilities for available solutions (Scopelliti et al., 2014) and investing in innovation. A higher level of financial resources enables uptake of multiple innovation projects, which affords an organisation greater flexibility and cross-fertilisation of ideas (Pichlak & Bratnicki, 2011).

While not strictly a resource, leaders or top managers play a significant role in promoting innovation by encouraging employees to pursue creative solutions and being open to new internally and externally produced knowledge (Pichlak & Bratnicki, 2011), making decisions on resource allocation for innovation implementation purposes and enabling strategic decisions (Damanpour & Schneider, 2006; Hameed & Counsell, 2014). These individuals usually wield the majority of decision-making capabilities, which makes them key to promoting innovation. The attitude of top managers towards innovation is not always positive, as some leaders may prefer standard methods and decisions, thus strongly impacting the uptake of innovative solutions in the organisation (Premkumar & Roberts, 1999).

The experts in the study by Pichlak (2015) support this view of top managers' crucial role in promoting innovation at every stage of innovation adoption, along with human resources. This applies to the number of qualified employees as well as top management's support of innovation implementation. Top managers enable the process of scanning the environment for innovative solutions during the initiation stage (Damanpour & Schneider, 2006); allocate resources during the decision adoption stage (Damanpour et al., 2009); and finally exert influence and authority to successfully implement innovation (Matta et al., 2012). In a similar vein, highly professional, qualified employees propose innovative solutions and efficient use of resources (Pichlak & Bratnicki, 2011). Interestingly, financial resources are seen as influential only at the decision adoption and implementation stages rather than the initiation stage. A higher allocated budget is much needed to speed up the decision-making process (Adams et al., 2006; Ahuja et al., 2008).

Another perspective from the innovation and organisational studies literature relevant to this resource perspective of antecedents of innovation adoption is that of dynamic capabilities (Eisenhardt & Martin, 2000; Teece et al., 1992, 1997). These are 'the means by which organizations alter the ways in which they make their living' (Helfat & Martin, 2015). The notion of dynamic capabilities is rooted in a resource-based view of organisations (Penrose, 1959), although this body of scholarship is primarily interested in how resources and capabilities contribute to firms' competitiveness. Nevertheless, dynamic capabilities are closely related to resources that enable innovation adoption.

Two components of dynamic capabilities – organisational and managerial – are especially pertinent to this discussion. Dynamic managerial capabilities are defined as 'the capabilities with which managers build, integrate, and reconfigure organizational resources and competences' (Adner & Helfat, 2003, 1012). Dynamic managerial capabilities have several components that are highly relevant to the organisational ability to innovate.

For example, organisations with absorptive capabilities, or 'the ability of a firm to recognize the value of new, external information, assimilate it, and apply it to commercial ends ... the ability to evaluate and utilize outside knowledge is largely a function of the level of prior knowledge' (Cohen & Levinthal, 1990, 128), demonstrate stronger ability of learning from partners, integrating external information and transforming it into embedded knowledge. Another dimension of dynamic managerial capabilities is innovative capability, which refers to an organisation's ability to develop innovative behaviours and processes aligned with strategic organisational goals (Wang & Ahmed, 2007).

In the same way as the three types of capacities required for BI institutional-isation – analytical, political and managerial capacities – organisational resources (Pichlak, 2015) and dynamic managerial capabilities (Eisenhardt & Martin, 2000; Teece et al., 1992, 1997) underpin organisational ability to integrate, reconfigure, renew and recreate its resources and capabilities in line with external changes. Therefore, we propose that the three capacities for BI institutionalisation, includ-ing organisational resources and a range of dynamic managerial capabilities, are a second precondition for effective institutionalisation of BI policy.

3.2.3 Experts in Public Management Innovation

New ideas and solutions require appropriate knowledge and expertise (Mumford, 2000); therefore, it is hardly surprising that knowledge, or expertise, has been found to influence innovative approaches to problem solving. Empirical links have been established between scientific productivity and work experience in the field (Simonton, 1988). The same applies to expertise or knowledge gained with experience, which is said to influence people's ability to come up with creative solutions to existing problems (Baer, 1998; Ericsson & Charness, 1994; Kulkarni & Simon, 1988).

The role of expertise of innovation, and specifically public sector innovation, has been discussed widely (Sorensen & Torfing, 2011). The experts are con-sidered a key node in the innovation network, and their role in the innovation adoption process is modulated by collaboration – there is a widely accepted view that innovation arises at the intersection of divergent knowledge domains (Pershina et al., 2019). A creative approach to combining diverse knowledge domains acts as a key driver of novel ideas and solutions.

The main challenge of collaborative innovation efforts lies in the tendency of expert communities belonging to different knowledge domains to form 'thought worlds', defined as 'a community of persons engaged in a certain domain of activity who have a shared understanding about that activity' (Dougherty, 1992, 182). Internally, thought worlds possess coherence and represent an area of specialty, with members sharing mutual understanding and distinct systems of meanings, beliefs, values and prescriptions, which serve as basis of professional recognition, identity and self-esteem (Carlile, 2004; Kaplan et al., 2017; Kellogg, 2014). However, this internal coherence contributes to challenges in communication and collaborative efforts whereby experts from distinct know-ledge domains perceive each other's approaches as less valuable due to a cognitive gap and knowledge fault lines (Dougherty & Dunne, 2012, 1470), conflicting goals and priorities and competition over resources (Holland et al., 2000). Moreover, professionals tend to develop their own specialised language and vocabulary, making it difficult for others to decipher (Edmondson & Nembhard, 2009).

Resolving these challenges is key for cross-knowledge domain collaborative innovation. The literature on innovation management offers two distinct approaches to solving this: knowledge integration and coordination. Thus, Okhuysen and Eisenhardt (2002) define the process of knowledge integration as the sharing and combining of individual expertise within a group to create new knowledge (371). In organisational sociology a different concept is used – that of coordination, which refers to integration of a set of interdependent and specialised tasks to realise a collective performance (Faraj & Xiao, 2006; Okhuysen & Bechky, 2009).

While a large share of the literature focuses on the managerial practices and governance structures (e.g. Grant, 1996; Ravasi & Verona, 2001), there is a literature stream that is concerned with the way of organising experts to manage the challenges of effective knowledge integration across boundaries. This includes such organisational support mechanisms as setup of cross-functional teams (Nonaka, 1994), or encouraging tasks and activities that enable knowledge integration, for example, prototyping and formal meetings (Clark et al., 1991).

The literature dedicated to the other perspective on resolving the challenges of cross-knowledge domain collaborative innovation – coordination – pays closer attention to the micro-dynamics of organising interaction among experts (Okhuysen & Bechky, 2009). The role of boundary-spanning digital and non-digital tools in facilitating collaboration 'on the ground' (Bechky, 2003; Nicolini et al., 2012; Star & Griesemer, 1989) has received special attention.

The role of experts in BI has also received some scholarly attention. There are multiple forms of expertise involved in design, production, and implementation of BI in public policy, from reliance on individual experts – academics, researchers in the fields of behavioural economics and psychology to epistemic communities (Simons & Schniedermann, 2021; Weible, 2018), multidisciplinary transnational knowledge brokers (Feitsma, 2018), among others. The role of knowledge brokers, like David Halpern of BIT is especially well researched and regarded as crucial for bridging the gap between research and practice and spreading the expertise globally. Knowledge brokers (Meyer, 2010) address the challenges of both knowledge integration and coordination and those of bridging the gap between science and policy which often arises due to complexity and conflict in this dyad. To diminish said gaps a professional group of knowledge brokers, with assigned role titles like 'diffusion fellows', 'knowledge transfer associates', and 'chief science officers' (Kislov et al., 2016) have gained popularity in recent years. The role of knowledge brokers lies in collection, diffusion and translation of evidence to ensure a smooth flow of information between policy-makers and researchers (Knight & Lyall, 2013). Kislov et al. (2016) describes the main tasks of knowledge brokers in the following terms: information management (gathering and transferring); linkage and exchange (networking); and facilitation in turning situated knowledge into action (transforming and facilitating) (Kislov et al., 2016; Ward et al., 2009). Experts as knowledge brokers are critical for effective institutionalisation of BI. Their role extends beyond simple utilisation of expertise to that of knowledge translation, communication and boundary-spanning activities that promote innovation adoption. To that end they organise themselves into special units between boundaries and engage in training, networking and tool-building (Feitsma, 2018).

3.3 Institutionalisation of BI through the Lens of Innovation Adoption

Based on our discussion so far, what emerges is a more systematic way of thinking about what is needed within governments to establish BI as a policy innovation. Three important conversations or common bridges exist within the policy design and policy innovation literatures in discussing the governance 'pre-conditions' that are needed in place for BI policy-making to develop over time.

- The first precondition has to do with procedural tools or organisational decisions.
- The second precondition has to do with the capacities and resources endowments for innovation adoption.
- The third precondition has to do with the role of specialists, subject-matter experts and managers both within government departments as well as external contracts/partnerships.

Figure 2 is a summary of the overlap in the conversations in policy design and policy innovation scholarship. Policy design literature offers various perspectives on the pre-conditions or capacities needed for policy-making. These, however, do share several features such as administrative capacity, sound political management, operational readiness in terms of resources, information, legal underpinnings, among others (Brenton et al., 2022; Howlett & Ramesh, 2016; Mukherjee et al., 2021; Saguin et al., 2018; Wu et al., 2015).

Policy innovation literature focuses heavily on organisational structure (Pichlak, 2015) and dynamic capabilities as essential for innovation adoption (Eisenhardt & Martin, 2000; Teece et al., 1992, 1997). Further, knowledge

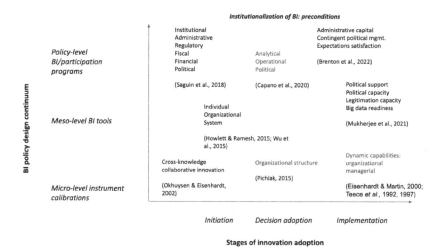

Figure 2 Conceptual overlaps in policy design and policy innovation literature

integration is given much attention as an important prerequisite for innovative solutions to take root (Okhuysen & Eisenhardt, 2002). The pattern of overlap is emerging when we look at these two scholarship streams together – analytical capacity or expertise; organisational/operational capacity or resources, legal arrangements, organisational scaffolding; and the intersection of organisational and political capacity or the ability to secure and sustain political support (Howlett & Ramesh, 2015; Wu et al., 2015).

Based on this pattern of overlap, we propose a theoretical framework for the institutionalisation of BI through three stages of innovation adoption, presented in Figure 3. Three types of capacities are needed for effective introduction and institutionalisation of BI in policy – analytical, organisational and political. Organisational and analytical capacities are more crucial at the initiation and decision adoption stages, while some organisational and political capacities are indispensable at the implementation stage.

4 Institutionalisation of BI in Policy: Australia, the Netherlands and Singapore

4.1 Methodology: Approach to Case Selection

In this section, we turn to three country cases that represent three distinct examples of a BI implementation journey with a focus on the three stages of innovation adoption and the level of policy design. The three country cases are Australia, the Netherlands and Singapore. All three consistently feature in conversations on BI policy adoption (World Bank, 2014) as examples par

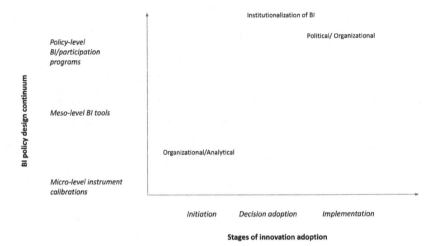

Figure 3 Theoretical framework

excellence. Each successful in their own right, these three examples are instrumental for our case for a differentiated approach to institutionalisation of BI
depending on the level of policy design and the stage of innovation adoption.

Our selection of these three cases is driven by the methodological approaches
discussed at length by Seawright and Gerring (2008). All three cases are
influential examples of BI application that can be characterised by high levels
of success and are often discussed in the context of effective BI implementation
(Ball & Head, 2021; Detenber, 2021; Feitsma & Schillemans, 2019). In addition, despite similar levels of success, these cases were selected using the 'most
different' criterion (Seawright & Gerring, 2008) due to the differences in the
level of BI intervention at which they were adopted. We rely on a range of
scholarly sources, as well as government reports and media coverage.

We expressly omit routinisation as a stage of innovation adoption when
presenting the three country cases. Routinisation, or 'automaticity in behavior,
typically including unintentionality, uncontrollability, lack of awareness, and
efficiency' (Ohly et al., 2006, 258), is an important stage in the innovation
adoption process; however, due to its association with established routines and
a certain degree of 'calcification' of processes, it might be too early to apply this
lens to BI adoption journeys in the country cases included in this Element.

4.2 Australia: The Structured Collaborative Approach

Even before Thaler and Sunstein's conceptualisation of 'nudge' became well
known, the ideas underpinning behavioural decision-making were influential in
some of the economic and regulatory agencies of the Australian government, as

well as in the health and human services agencies, since at least 2007. For example, the Australian Department of Finance had a long-standing interest in 'better practice' regulation and voluntary codes of compliance, while the Australian Tax Office (ATO) had explored behavioural issues concerning tax evasion and tax compliance (Jones et al., 2021).

One of the early adopters of BI insights in policy, Australia was largely influenced by the success of the UK's Behavioural Insights Team (BIT), which prompted its government at the state level to forge links with BIT and start experimenting with micro-level instrument calibrations. This evolved into solutions for more complex policy problems, culminating in the establishment of a behavioural policy unit at the central government level with an emphasis on identifying low-cost measures to influence behavioural change.

The projects undertaken by the central government BI unit, Behavioural Economics Team Australia (BETA), and similar units in other government departments (see Box 2), reveal a broad cross-section of activities, including strengthening the resilience of students, dealing with cyber security, improving census participation, the workplace experience of apprentices, improving support for drought-affected farmers, improving consumer engagement with electricity retailers and managing unconscious bias in public sector recruitment practices (DPM&C Australia, 2023).

BOX 2 AUSTRALIAN DEPARTMENT OF JOBS AND SMALL BUSINESS (DoJB) EXAMPLE

DJSB is currently progressing a number of trials. In 2016, the department worked in partnership with the UK BIT and jobactive (employment services portal) provider Mission Providence to co-design and implement a behavioural economics trial with the aim of increasing the take-up of Australian government wage subsidies. Wage subsidies are payments made by the Australian government to encourage businesses to employ eligible job seekers. A report on the results of this trial was published on the department's website in February 2018. According to DJSB, the trial led to an increase in the number of wage subsidy agreements signed. In addition, feedback received during the trial led to the fine-tuning of the final design and implementation of policy changes, announced in the 2016 Australian government budget and implemented nationally on 1 January 2017. The DJSB behavioural economics team provides department-wide advice, regularly promotes behavioural economics both within and outside the department and participates in an Australian Public Service (APS)-wide behavioural economics practitioners network.

At the state level, the range of projects implemented with the help of BI is also extensive, from childhood obesity, outpatient appointments, and applications for jobs in rural areas, to participation in justice programmes, improving public sector diversity, improving the success of return to work programmes and boosting productivity (NSW Behavioural Insights Unit, 2020).

4.2.1 Initiation

Australia, along with Singapore, was an early mover in setting up behavioural teams for policy-making in the government. The combination of the ideas articulated in books such as *Nudge* and the steady stream of practical trial results from the UK's BIT was particularly intriguing to pragmatic public administrators in these countries.

Interestingly, state initiatives in Australia on BI application in policy preceded the creation of a central government unit. Both state initiatives – in New South Wales (NSW) and Victoria – evolved out of partnerships with the BIT in the United Kingdom. For example, a BI unit in NSW was created in 2012 after a partnership project with BIT UK, having started with micro-level instrument calibrations such as redesigning notices of fine payments, decreasing the number of missed hospital appointments and so forth (Ball & Head, 2021). This later developed into policy-level programme operations that sought to solve more complex problems, for example childhood obesity and domestic violence. In Victoria, a collaboration with the UK colleagues took the form of the director of BIT UK acting as the lead thinker in a series of workshops, as well as establishing a community of practice aimed at designing behavioural trials for the Health Promotion Foundation between 2014 and 2016.

4.2.2 Decision Adoption

Not much information is available on the impetus of the decision to establish a central government BI unit, which was created in 2016. At the same time, according to Ball et al. (2017), the interest in BI for policy was on the rise in federal government agencies long before the establishment of the formal unit. Most sources, however, mention the success of the BIT in the United Kingdom as an important driving factor for experimenting with BI in policy at the state level, followed by the establishment of a formal central government unit. According to the World Bank, initial support has grown rapidly, and BETA was supported by thirteen partner agencies in February 2016 when the team was launched. This can be labelled as a 'policy transfer' (Dolowitz & Marsh, 2000) of sorts; however, a more detailed account of the process other than the desire to emulate BIT UK's success is not immediately available.

Recruiting appropriate staff is a major concern for BI unit managers. The available skill sets influence their capacity to manage project challenges. Technical skills in such fields as economics, statistics and cognitive psychology are popular choices. Specialised fields such as neuropsychology are also occasionally present. Public sector project management experience is seen as a valuable skill for these units. An appreciation of public sector culture plays a key role in the successful steering and implementation of projects. The capacity of individual practitioners to work in project-based teams, usually with other partner agencies, is also critical.

The Behavioural Economics Team Australia has an online course titled 'BI for Public Policy', aimed at public servants who would like to learn more about BI and start applying it in their jobs. In addition, there is the Behavioural Insights Practitioners' Network coordinated by BETA. This provides a forum for existing behavioural insights practitioners across the APS to meet and hear from colleagues in other agencies, share their experiences and develop their understanding of emerging trends in behavioural economics.

4.2.3 Implementation

The Behavioural Economics Team Australia is a joint initiative funded by nineteen federal government departments and agencies. Its business model requires co-funding of project costs by other federal government partners. This shared, collaborative approach was unlike any other model at the time. The staff is seconded from the participating agencies and chosen according to a wide range of criteria, from area of expertise to years of experience, in both the public service and beyond. This allowed BETA to build both behavioural economics capability across the APS but also internal capacity at the same time.

During its first two years of operation, BETA relied principally upon Harvard professor Michael Hiscox, the founding director, for academic expertise and advice on research design. Since mid 2017, University of Sydney professor Robert Slonim has provided that expertise and guidance for the team. Since 2018, BETA has been evolving and expanding its relationships with academia by establishing an Academic Advisory Panel. The panel will provide expert advice from scholars working on the frontiers of behavioural science and create opportunities for collaborations between researchers and BETA.

Behavioural Economics Team Australia projects are funded from the government's Modernisation Fund, designed to enhance public sector innovation and contributions from partner agencies. This approach to funding the BI in policy is well aligned with our argument that BI is essentially a form of innovation, and hence our reliance on a framework pertaining to stages of innovation adoption is an appropriate approach.

4.2.4 Lessons Learnt from the Australian Case

Figure 4 illustrates how stages of innovation adoption interact with the policy framework in Australia. As we have discussed in this case, BI adoption in Australia is focused heavily on application to policy-level BI, including national programmes tackling wicked problems such as health, tax compliance, employment policy, social policy interventions, market competition and so forth.

Most of the work undertaken for BI application has sought to apply experimental methods, such as randomised control trials (RCT), which is in line with the skillsets of the staff in most BI units across the government departments. This is also consistent with the influence of the UK BIT, which has conducted over 400 RCTs, trials and projects, meaning that RCTs are seen by Australian policy practitioners as most capable of providing robust evidence for policy innovation and assessing the relative efficacy of options.

We use the example of wage subsidies project by DoJB from Box 1 to illustrate the approach to BI adoption in Australia at the policy level. At the initiation stage, co-design of the intervention takes place with relevant stakeholders. This is followed by a launch of the RCT or trial at the decision adoption stage. The results of the trial are available publicly to secure support and ensure

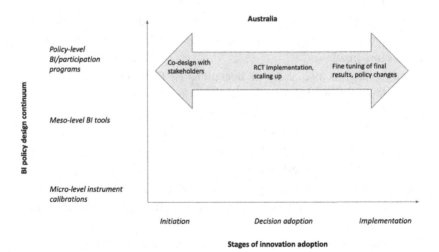

Figure 4 Policy design continuum and stages of innovation adoption in Australia

transparency of the proposed intervention. Feedback is received at this stage that is instrumental for further refining the intervention. Finally, at the implementation stage the results are carefully calibrated in line with the feedback and policy changes are proposed for implementation.

In terms of capacities, the commitment to analytical capacity, as expressed in BETA's efforts to recruit experts, build thought communities, share expertise between departments and provide tools for training, was especially evident at the initiation and decision adoption stages (Ball et al., 2017; Ball & Head, 2021). At this time, importance was placed on creating an impetus for a more centralised approach to BI after the success at the state level. This helped bring the issues of funding and securing the federal government's support for a centralised unit to the fore later, at the implementation stage. The Behavioural Economics Team Australia enjoyed relatively quick development into an influential government unit with the requisite financial resources due to the ability of the interested government agencies to build analytical and organisational capacities at earlier stages of policy adoption.

4.3 The Netherlands: The Networked, Bottom-Up Approach

As with many governments around the world, the Dutch state has been influenced by behavioural insights for several decades (Rose, 1998). However, policy-makers started taking a focused interest in BI for policy only around 2008. This growing interest resulted in a symposium proposed by the Scientific Council for Government Policy (Wetenschappelijke Raad voor het Regeringsbeleid (WRR)). The symposium was aimed at exploring the potential uses of BI in policy-making. The WRR symposium was an attempt to follow in the footsteps of other country governments, such as the United Kingdom and the United States in their efforts to engage with the behavioural sciences. In the case of the Netherlands, however, the uptake of BI in public policy was met with some academic, bureaucratic and ethical resistance that prevented early discussions from evolving into tangible steps.

Nevertheless, these early discussions culminated in the creation in 2012 of the first BI unit in the Dutch government. This small unit was formed in the Ministry of Infrastructure and Environment, initially with only two staff members. At the same time, some efforts were undertaken to form a more coordinated engagement effort to utilise BI in public policy-making. The impetus for this development can be attributed to three main reasons. First was the much lauded effort of the UK's BIT (Halpern, 2015b).[4] Secondly, 2012 saw the emergence after the election of a Liberal and Labour coalition government headed by Mark Rutte. The coalition, founded upon the principles of liberalism but also forged in a time of austerity, found the low cost and libertarian nature of BI appealing. Thirdly, this time also saw the emergence of an opportune political environment for policy experimentation.

The eventual institutionalisation of BI for policy-making in the Netherlands was preceded by extensive discussions of how this could be achieved in the most effective way. The Ministry of Economic Affairs lobbied for the formation of a central BIT that would mirror the structure of the UK's BIT. This, however, raised several concerns. Firstly, it was not immediately clear which government department would host such a unit. This is because the structure of Dutch government departments is non-hierarchical, where no department has direct control over others. Second, an argument was put forward that a single BI unit would become an easy target for the BI doubters, giving them an easy argument that BI are excessively centralised.

It was out of this discussion that the Behavioural Insights Network Netherlands (BIN NL) was eventually formed. The network has representatives from all ministries and facilitates knowledge sharing about the application of BI to policy-making and its implementation, supervision and communication.

More recently, the Information Council (Voorlichtingsraad), which formulates the joint communication policy of the central government for the Prime Minister and the ministries, started a government-wide trial behaviour lab for communication in 2017. As of 2018, the cabinet continues to advocate for the strengthening of BI at the departmental level and for BIN NL to continue working to bring departments together. Behavioural insights have also been incorporated into the government Integral Assessment Framework for Policy and Regulations, published by the Ministry of Justice and Security, to guide policy-makers on instruments and guidelines to formulate policies and regulations.

The types of projects implemented by BIN NL are wide-ranging; however, the emphasis is on instruments that have small- to medium-level effect, such as communication tweaks and incorporation of behavioural considerations in analysis or policy-making, through to the widespread implementation of policies based on experimentation utilising BI. Examples include specific messages and reminders, advertisements, field experiments and financial incentives, among others. Box 3 is an example of such measures that focus on overcoming the limits to rational behaviour through regulation, understanding context and barriers to certain behaviours, 'budging' beliefs and attitudes and presenting opportunities for testing desirable attitudes and behaviours. Thus, the level of engagement with BI in the Netherlands can be characterised as mostly 'meso'.

BOX 3 THE DUTCH EXAMPLE

The Ministry of Infrastructure and Water Management applied BI to the design of a policy programme titled 'Optimising Use', aimed at improving mobility, enhancing use of public transport and encouraging flexible work arrangements. This policy programme aims to improve accessibility in twelve of the busiest urban regions of the country through a package of concrete and quantifiable measures that focus on the needs and behaviour of travellers and transport providers. These solutions are customised for each region in collaboration with local businesses, conditional on co-financing.

Measures include 'shove'-like instruments that remove barriers to desirable behaviour, such as building more bicycle shelters at stations, providing better, readily available travel information, shorter waiting times at docks, reliable sailing times and discounted e-bikes for personnel. The regional programmes involve a special component: the 'smart deals', or arrangements with local businesses aimed at reducing employee travel during rush hour by means of tax measures, e-bike campaigns and options for flexible working.

4.3.1 Initiation

The Dutch government's interest in BI was signalled in 2008 when the WRR held a symposium on the use of BI for policy-making. The Dutch government may have started expressing interest in BI following successful examples of other countries' experimentation with BI tools, for example those in the United Kingdom and the United States. At the same time, this stage didn't lead to formal decision-making on BI adoption until 2012.

4.3.2 Decision Adoption

In 2012 a small unit was formed in the Dutch Ministry of Infrastructure and Environment with only two staff members. Yet again, the success of the UK BIT has served as an impetus to realising the interest in BI first expressed in the 2008 WRR symposium. The institutionalisation of BI was supported by stand-alone parts of the civil service, located in various departments, with full and formal political support coming later.

A major driving force for the coordinated use of BI across public policy in the Netherlands has come from the government's Interdepartmental Strategy Network. The members of this strategy network are civil servants who meet regularly to discuss new policy ideas and initiatives. Proposed by several different ministries, an interdepartmental BI initiative was established that would eventually become BIN NL. Thus, the decision-making process was rather bottom-up, ensuring that government departments had a stake in the creation of BI units rather than following the orders of the leadership.

4.3.3 Implementation

Behavioural insights have been institutionalised in the Dutch government as a network, which is reflected in its name – Behavioural Insights Network Netherlands (BIN NL). The network has representatives from all government departments with an aim of facilitating effective knowledge sharing about the application of BI to policy-making, implementation, supervision and communication. More recently, in 2017, the Information Council (Voorlichtingsraad), which is responsible for the joint communication policy of the central government, started a trial government-wide BI lab for communication. The cabinet continues to experiment with BI at the departmental level and for BIN NL to continue working to bring departments together.

4.3.4 Lessons Learnt from the Dutch Case

Recent analyses of the emergence of BI in the Netherlands indicate that there has been an ongoing process of contestation and politicisation of behavioural expertise (see https://journals.sagepub.com/doi/10.1177/2399654419867711; Feitsma, 2018). The contestation of expertise has in part been a product of the inevitable decisions that must be made in relation to which forms of expertise, with which particular behavioural insights, should be engaged with. It has also been a result of the process of working out which forms of behavioural expertise are actually most relevant to the policy-making process itself (Feitsma, 2018b). Furthermore, the institutionalisation of expertise is not about bringing scientists into government, as it is governmental officials actively filtering scientific insights to meet their own needs (Feitsma, 2018b). It is thus clear that the emergence of BPP in the Netherlands has not so much involved the hardwiring of behavioural science expertise into government but rather the training and repurposing of existing civil servants in new policy-making skills (Feitsma & Schillemans, 2019). In addition, the Dutch example is illustrative of a bottom-up approach predicated on limited resources and weak links to policy-makers and institutional actors, which translated to uncertain support from key government actors and the constant need of BI experts to defend their legitimacy until the gains became clearer, as reflected in the growing global recognition of BI tools and a rise in prominence of epistemic communities and knowledge brokers (Feitsma & Schillemans, 2019).

Figure 5 Illustrates how stages of innovation adoption interact with the policy framework in the Netherlands. Behavioural insight adoption in the Netherlands places emphasis on meso-level instruments, or 'thinks' such as developing an understanding of what drives human behaviour through RCTs, tweaking communication instruments, or 'shoves' aimed at changing behaviour by removing barriers and creating incentives (Afif et al., 2019).

We use the example of the 'Optimising Use' project from Box 3 to illustrate the approach to BI adoption in the Netherlands at the meso level. At the initiation stage, research is carried out that aims at identifying barriers to and enablers of the desirable user behaviour, done through surveys, interviews and analysis of the existing user data, among others approaches. This is followed by communicating with interested stakeholders and engaging in co-production with non-government actors at the decision adoption stage to secure additional resources for implementation and enhance legitimacy and participation. The solutions are aimed at budging existing beliefs that lead to unwanted behaviours. The resulting ideas are sent to a trial stage to ensure the workability of the proposed intervention. At the implementation stage, a clear and detailed communication campaign is used as the main driver.

The Netherlands example is also a good illustration of the need for analytical, organisational and political capacities to be built at different stages of policy adoption. Analytical capacity or expertise was a major focus of the government departments, who emphasised drawing on BI expert knowledge across departments to be shared widely through BIN NL. Organisational arrangements and

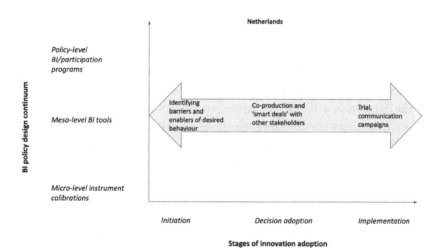

Figure 5 Policy design continuum and stages of innovation adoption in the Netherlands

political support for a more formal approach to using BI in policy came later, at the implementation stage, when a BI lab was proposed for implementation in 2017 to cement the use of BI in policy in a more centralised fashion.

4.4 Singapore: A Networked but Centrally Sponsored Approach

Singapore is another example of an early adopter of BI in policy with a high rate of success and recognition. From its earliest days as a nation, Singapore has enacted many measures to try to get its citizens to behave 'properly'. Among the early policies set out were heterogenous public housing estates (i.e., state-mandated integration), mother tongue language requirements in schools and moving food vendors off the streets into regulated spaces. These social developments, coupled with economic progress, allowed Lee to claim that Singapore had gone from a third world to a first world country in the span of a generation (Lee, 2012).

However, the true BI revolution was catalysed by the success of the BIT team in the United Kingdom, much like in Australia. Unlike the United Kingdom, the application of behavioural sciences in Singapore's public policy did not begin with a big bang driven from the centre. Instead, it was a ground-up movement, with various agencies exploring and experimenting with small-scale projects. The first teams started out as 'skunk works' (Soon, 2017), learning the techniques while scrounging for willing partners prepared to give these new approaches a try. Quick wins were needed to gain confidence and win support from senior management.

Today, with over 250 members in a community of practice across fifty public agencies, the use of BI in Singapore public policy has evolved from an initial fascination with how cognitive biases challenge the traditional way of designing policies, to a more sophisticated framework of testing and accumulating insights on behavioural interventions. This shift has also shown that the use of BI is more than improving the last mile experience of citizens – it has the potential to fundamentally challenge the way we think about government policies and programmes.

The domains in which the Singapore government successfully implemented BI are numerous – from finance, health, and public utilities to environment, transport and, public communications, among others (see Box 4).

4.4.1 Initiation

Singapore's experiments with BI began even before it established its first BI unit in one of the line ministries. As far back as the 1960s, Singapore utilised a behavioural approach to tweaking citizens' behaviour in such areas as public cleanliness, family planning and donation of organs. Although not technically 'nudges', these policies did aim to modify citizens' behaviour to attain policy goals.

BOX 4 SINGAPORE'S MINISTRY OF MANPOWER EXAMPLE

One of the trials conducted by the Ministry of Manpower's (MOM) Work Pass Division and the Central Provident Fund Board was to nudge employers of foreign domestic workers to make timely levy payments. For employers who defaulted, MOM sent them a letter to remind them to make payment. In the trial, a randomly selected half of 1,000 people received the usual monthly letter on white paper. The other half received a letter on pink paper that had a simplified layout, containing clearer important information in addition to the social norm that 96 per cent of the employers pay their levies on time. The pink letter was intended to invoke the norm of overdue bill notices sent by telecommunications and utility companies and reinforce the message that the due levy payment was late. The pink letters resulted in an increase in compliance of 3 per cent to 5 per cent, which was equivalent to $1.5 million more in levies collected.

However, the formal recognition of BI as a policy tool was brought about in Singapore, just like in Australia, by the developments in the United Kingdom. Unlike the United Kingdom, the application of behavioural insights in Singapore public policy did not emanate from the centre. Instead, it was a ground-up movement, with various agencies exploring on a small scale. The first teams in agencies would learn the techniques while looking for potential partners prepared to serve as testbeds. This was done partially to secure support from senior management by demonstrating successful experimentation initiatives.

One of the earliest examples of this approach was the introduction of the 'Save Water Campaign' in 2005, which used behavioural insights to encourage Singaporeans to conserve water. The campaign used various tactics such as social norms, feedback and incentives to nudge people into changing their behaviour, and it was highly successful, resulting in a significant reduction in water consumption. Singapore prefers a 'nudge not shove' approach to attaining the desired behaviour (Public Service Division, 2014) as more cost-effective and easier to implement.

4.4.2 Decision Adoption

The first BI unit was established in the Ministry of Environment and Water Resources in 2011. The following year, the Ministry of Communications and Information began BI in a bid to follow the government's imperative to move towards data-driven communications. In 2017, the Singapore Public Service expressed full commitment to continuing the integration of BI in policy to improve lives in Singapore. Behavioural insights within the Singaporean government now take place primarily at the agency level, with at least fifteen government agencies utilising BI in their policy-making processes. This approach is highly networked rather than centralised and recognises the ability of departments to make their own decisions regarding the application of BI (Afif et al., 2019).

Political commitment has been a critical factor in the success of behavioural insights in Singapore. The government has demonstrated a strong commitment to using behavioural insights to improve policy outcomes, and this has been reflected in the allocation of resources, establishment of dedicated teams and integration of behavioural insights into policy-making (Afif et al., 2019).

4.4.3 Implementation

Since their inception, BI teams in various government agencies have worked on a wide range of initiatives, including encouraging healthier eating habits, promoting financial literacy and improving labour market outcomes. Behavioural insight units have also collaborated with other government agencies and private sector partners to develop and test new interventions, and many of these interventions have been highly successful. In addition, government agencies rely on collaborations with academia as well as private sector consultants as conduits for new BI expertise. In addition, the Civil Service College serves as a platform for policy-makers, academics and practitioners to exchange ideas and share knowledge about behavioural insights. The Civil Service College organises events, workshops and seminars to promote the use of behavioural insights in policy-making (Detenber, 2021).

Behavioural insights are used to inform the design of policies and programmes to achieve better outcomes. For instance, the Singapore government used behavioural insights to design the 'opt-out' organ donation programme. Instead of requiring people to actively opt-in to the programme, the default option was set to be 'opt-in', resulting in a significant increase in the number of registered donors.

Randomised controlled trials (RCTs) are often used to test the effectiveness of behavioural interventions in Singapore. For example, a pilot programme was launched in 2017 to provide households with real-time feedback on their electricity consumption, which resulted in a 6 per cent reduction in electricity usage. The pilot was subsequently scaled up and made available to all households in Singapore.

The Singapore government has collaborated with private sector organisations to implement behavioural interventions. For example, the Health Promotion Board partnered with supermarkets to display healthier food options more prominently, resulting in an increase in sales of healthy food items.

Digital platforms such as mobile apps and websites are increasingly being employed to implement behavioural interventions in Singapore. For example, the 'National Steps Challenge' is a government-led initiative that encourages Singaporeans to adopt a more active lifestyle through a mobile app that tracks their physical activity and provides incentives for achieving certain goals. The Singapore government also uses data analytics to understand people's behaviour and design policies that address their needs. For example, the government uses data on people's travel patterns to improve public transportation services and reduce congestion.

4.4.4 Lessons Learnt from the Singaporean Case

A positive outlook towards adoption of BI is common among policy-makers and public administrators. They recognise, however, that there are ethical issues and practical concerns when using BI, as well as limits to nudging. Hence, the civil servants regard the approach not as a panacea but as a resource to be thoughtfully applied. As the Deputy Secretary (Development) in the Ministry of Manpower put it, 'BI is not a silver bullet' (Kok, n.d., 110). Behavioural insights are implemented in Singapore through a variety of approaches, including policy design, experimentation and partnerships with private sector organisations.

Figure 6 illustrates how stages of innovation adoption interact with the policy framework in Singapore. Behavioural insight adoption in Singapore places emphasis on micro-level interventions, both those aimed at encouraging mindful choice and those tackling attentional shifts (Detenber, 2021).

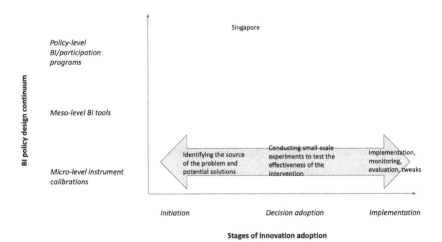

Figure 6 Policy design continuum and stages of innovation adoption in Singapore

We use the example of MOM's Work Pass Division example from Box 4 to illustrate the approach to BI adoption for micro-level interventions in Singapore. At the initiation stage, research is carried out aimed at identifying the source of the problem and potential solutions through surveys, interviews and analysis of user data, among others. This is followed by rigorous experimentation to test the effectiveness of behavioural interventions before implementing them on a larger scale. This approach has helped to identify effective interventions and avoid wasting resources on ineffective ones. The solutions are deployed and regularly monitored for effectiveness, making implementation and improvement an iterative process.

Analytical capacity is at the heart of Singapore's approach to staffing its government. Singapore is world-famous for offering its public servants competitive salaries. Hiring experts with extensive knowledge of BI and collaborating with academia was the priority at the initiation and decision adoption stages, as well as setting the stage for a networked approach to BI with departments making their own decisions on how to approach the organisational and resource endowment of BI in policy. At the implementation stage, government agencies in Singapore make sure to secure public and political support prior to rolling out the initiative.

4.5 Additional Considerations

This section aimed to analyse the experience of the three frontrunners in BI institutionalisation with application of BI at three different levels of policy instruments. While this Element assumes a neutral, apolitical approach in describing the cases in order to highlight the procedural factors and, specifically, the capacities and resources needed to successfully adopt and implement BI, it would be remiss to not at least discuss some important contextual considerations that contribute to BI implementation. After all, Thaler and Sunstein (2009) note that 'there is no such thing as a "neutral" design' (40). Following are some of the important political factors that underscore the essential conversation governments need to be having around adopting BI, beyond capacities and resources.

Firstly, two out of three cases described are from settings that can be depicted as varying shades of paternalistic, which is hardly surprising given that Thaler and Sunstein (2009) describe this brand of behavioural approach as 'libertarian paternalism'. More discussion is needed on how BI would fare in settings that are on the other end of the scale and find any restrictions of freedom of choice unsavoury, and especially what this would mean for the type of capacities needed for adoption and implementation.

Secondly, out of the perceived limits placed on citizens' autonomy and liberty justifiably come ethical concerns with BI application. Attitudes of the public have to be well understood and factored in. Seen by some commentators as manipulation or even coercion (Hausman & Welch, 2010), either BI needs to be repackaged to be more palatable to the public or their benefits need to be articulated along with potential side-effects and how the government is planning to mitigate them. The issue of information asymmetry and availability needs to be solved before BI is used as a policy solution. Whether this would need to be factored into the conversation on capacities merits a separate discussion.

Thirdly, to avoid selective reading of the application of BI, policy-makers need to have a clear idea of the impact of BI application on not just individual behaviour but also legal institutions and mechanisms (Lepenies & Malecka, 2015). Nudges are non-normative because they are not legally prescriptive regarding how people should behave. Hence comes the debate on the most effective way to reconcile the application of BI with potential questions around their legitimacy.

Finally, additional contextual variables to be considered include administrative contexts, policy transfer culture, advisory systems and regulatory traditions. This Element is the first effort in trying to understand the procedural tools needed for effective BI adoption and implementation and could be the first step towards an informed discussion in this regard.

5 Towards a Consistent Framework for BI in Policy Design

There is no dearth in the literature when it comes to evaluating the effectiveness of BI in policy-making in various domains and sectors, the specific policy structures and techniques to ensure successful implementation or the role of epistemic communities in promoting BI, among others. Furthermore, the overall body of literature concerning BI tools is characterised by a divide between academic scholarship and practitioner-oriented literature, such as government and consulting reports, working papers and books published by international organisations, OECD and the World Bank.

Given this divide, there is scant generalisable knowledge on the administrative necessities and capacities needed by the government for the effective design of BI tools (Kuehnhanss, 2019). The academic literature is still more preoccupied with discussing the instrumental content of BI policy rather than the procedural requirements or the relevant conducive environments needed for the inclusion of BI to be a deliberate, knowledge-informed policy-making endeavour. At the other end of the spectrum are those insights rooted in practice – government and international organisations produce reports that are often exploratory in nature, based purely on the lived experiences of BI units. These reports are studies of BI rather than encompassing efforts to combine with the normative foundations of how to make BI innovation in the government take off. This makes it hard to resist the interpretation that academics in the field follow rather than lead or collaborate with practitioners: practice informs research with little cross-pollination.

The most manifest aspect of this divide is the academic literature's propensity to fail to offer generalised, theoretical knowledge about how norm-based or BI policy solutions are designed and implemented through new and existing policy programmes. While the practice-oriented output produced by governments, international organisations and external experts does to some extent engage in such analysis, their prescriptions and recommendations are based on what has already been implemented in specific cases, rather than on the larger body of comparative research on public policy and administration surrounding institutional prerequisites and the necessary capacities for policy implementation.

This gap is also apparent in other aspects of BI literature, from evaluations of existing BI intervention designs to the most common challenges of effective BI implementation (Battaglio Jr. et al., 2019; Hallsworth & Kirkman, 2020; Halpern, 2015a; John, 2018; Shafir, 2013). Most recommendations stemming from these studies, again, focus on substantive tool aspects such as the choice of architecture and the viable strategies to manipulate it in order to achieve the desired policy outcomes. Monographs and edited volumes on the topic have been published that discuss the application of BI in various policy areas, such as health care, finance, education, public transport and so forth (Low, 2011; Oliver, 2015; Ruggeri, 2018, among others). In this regard, the OECD has been especially prolific, drawing on cases and examples from its member countries and demonstrating best practices in action. What remains missing is a procedural angle to these discussions.

The exposition presented in this Element has aimed to distil generalisable lessons on how a growing interest in BI in policy-making is leading to patterns of organisational adaptations within governments. Questions arise thereafter about whether and to what extent modifications made to a government's own internal procedural functions and instruments in response to more BI-centred work are having an impact on the substantive design of policy instruments. The growing literature on behavioural public policy indicates that a certain degree of isomorphism is involved in how the assumptions made about human behaviour are resulting in similar kinds of experiments and studies to be commissioned, with similar expertise in behavioural insights research at the policy formulation stages. That is, the growth of behavioural expertise within the government can follow arrangements (such as BITs) that are either time delimited and contracted out or more quasi-permanent internal departments or divisions within relevant ministries and agencies (Mukherjee & Giest, 2020).

At the same time, in the constellation of political actors who are involved in the process of policy formulation, there is growing evidence that BITs occupy the unique position of being, on the one hand, subject-matter experts who contribute to the knowledge and information that is used in policy-making; on the other hand, owing to their specialised expertise, BITs can also perform the role of design decision makers with significant say in the structure and content of policy instruments designed based on behavioural insights. In contemporary policy formulation situations, BITs have been instrumental as activators of policy designs that are specifically aimed at bringing about modest yet measurable modifications in the actions of the public towards prosocial / pro-environmental behaviours through the use of 'nudges' and other behavioural cues. Without the use of traditional instruments, such mechanisms are able to stimulate nearly subconscious compliance with government directives, using not necessarily government's resources of coercion, law enforcement or fiscal means, but rather their organisational and analytical endowments (Howlett, 2018).

As surmised by Thaler and Sunstein (2009), the managerial and technical work of 'a choice architect includes the responsibility for organizing the context in which people make decisions . . . there is no such thing as a "neutral" design' (1). Almost contradictorily, nudges have gained a reputation of being 'fast and furious' (Haynes et al., 2012), policy elements that can be readily custom-designed and added to existing policy mixes (Benartzi et al., 2017). The procedural capacities needed to deliver a nudge through 'processes of designing, testing and implementing nudge interventions are far more complicated, which questions the supposed "efficiency" of nudges' (De Ridder et al., 2020, 161).

What does this say about the relative power of behavioural work and expertise within government and the sway it wields regarding the content of policy design? Furthermore, are enough patterns of influence discernible such that conjectures can be drawn about their effect on policy change over the longer term? Nudges, for example, are often shown to be counterproductive to environmental regulations already in place. However, a significant investment of public monies in BI research for policy-making may commit to pathways of influence towards the institutionalising of what is currently considered an innovation.

5.1 Organisational Adaptations

Through the empirical exposition presented in this Element, what is clearly evident is that the position of a dedicated behavioural insights unit within a government ministry or agency can have a significant impact on how behavioural insights are formulated as well as implemented. What is also evident, especially in the aftermath of the global COVID-19 pandemic, is that this impact can be diverse depending on its manifestation related to the content of policy tools functioning across different sectors and focal areas. For example, according to the World Health Organization (WHO), behavioural units or behavioural research units that were set up in Europe in response to COVID-19 performed a variety of tasks ranging from scaling up cultural behavioural and media activities across agencies relevant to health and welfare (e.g. Cultural, Behavioural and Media Insights Centre [CUBE], Government of Finland), to more specifically and only dealing with national COVID-19 responses and their behavioural implications (e.g. Corona Behavior Unit, Netherlands). For both of these examples the actual tasks taken on by the BI unit in delivering BI projects may be very similar, with the difference lying only in the sector and the scale. Distilling the cases studied in this Element, Figure 7 shows the four main phases undertaken in the design and delivery of a typical BI project. As such, the capacities and capabilities housed within a BI unit need to reflect (1) skills related to problem framing and prioritising policy goals; (2) research and monitoring skills related to analysis of individual behaviour social norms as well as historical trajectories of policy design; (3) technical skills related to methods of designing pilots, randomised controlled trials and intervention design; (4) evaluation skills related to impact evaluation and monitoring of evidence that is being generated about the process outcomes and impacts of proposed behavioural interventions and any unexpected repercussions, and (5) political and stakeholder management skills to scale up projects with proof of concept and do so successfully through political and social buy-in.

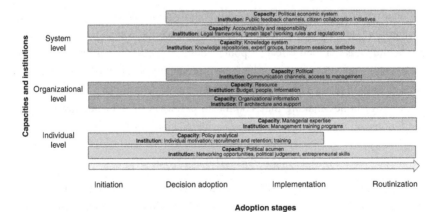

Figure 7 Policy capacities and the institutionalisation of BI policy design

These capacities further need to coordinate action in order to plan and secure resources for the perpetuity of activities generated by the unit.

In doing so, the presence of a behavioural unit can permeate different phases of the policy-making process, and its flexibility or 'nimbleness' in being able to adapt to the various phases of policy-making can become a significant indicator of its tenure within the government.

So, how does this flexibility translate to strategic organisational decisions that must be taken when instating a behavioural unit within the government? Beyond project and programme design, behavioural units have been shown to have a critical role in delivering policy advice. Most often this advice has to do with building not just a behavioural tool in isolation from other existing policy tools but also one that is meant to complement and enhance the work of existing policy toolkits. As mentioned before, the literature on policy design and behavioural insights finds that nudges in the most general sense are rarely stand-alone instruments being implemented; instead, they tend to be situated in a larger implementation context that includes existing regulations as well as potentially counteracting behavioural interventions deployed by private stakeholders (Ekhardt & Wieding, 2016). Therefore, in providing behavioural policy advice for existing policy portfolios, the behavioural unit's role goes beyond analytical and technical capabilities for programme design, to one that approaches the role of knowledge brokering and traversing the science–policy divide.

5.2 Remaining Puzzles

An alignment with context represents the cornerstone of effective policy design. While the consideration of the influence of social and community norms is treated as foundational through different implementation contexts, specific attention to behaviourally informed instrument components in policy design is a relatively new phenomenon. Many policy instruments have behavioural assumptions as part of their foundation in order 'to get people to do things they might not otherwise do or enable people to do things that they might not have done otherwise' (Schneider & Ingram, 1990, 513). Such considerations become especially pertinent, as evinced through the outcomes of a global public health crisis such as COVID-19.

As reiterated in this Element, despite their seeming embeddedness, the conceptual treatment of behavioural tools within the scholarship of policy instruments has remained piecemeal even though behavioural insights have been seen to inspire a wide variety of policy responses. These responses have been defined differently in the literature depending on whether researchers take on the narrower view of nudging or the wider scope of 'thinks' in BI, which galvanise more sustained and deliberative participation in the policy process. As surmised by scholars navigating behavioural public policy and policy instrument studies, 'the spectrum of behavioral policy instruments is large, including efforts of political and administrative simplification to reduce the cognitive burden on citizens, education programmes for decisions under the conditions of risk and insecurity, techniques of social norms marketing, and behaviorally informed regulation' (Strassheim & Beck, 2019, 3).

As the examples presented in this Element indicate, there is a need to organise the sheer diversity of behavioural means in terms of their place in the policy process. Some work towards this end has begun in line with distinguishing between policy instrument components that are 'behaviourally-tested (i.e. initiatives based on an ad-hoc test, or scaled out after an initial experiment), or behaviourally-informed (i.e. initiatives designed explicitly on previously existing behavioural evidence), or behaviourally-aligned (initiatives that, at least a posteriori, can be found to be in line with behavioural evidence)' (Ciriolo et al., 2019, 6). Nudges, in this reasoning, fall into the last category of behaviourally aligned initiatives as these represent instrument calibrations by simplifying and framing of information; making changes to the physical environment in which information is presented; manipulating the default policy option; and the use of social norms, which need not always emanate from dedicated experiments or randomised controlled trials but may rather constitute a 'what works' principle on the ground during policy implementation.

That is, behavioural means working in policy toolkits dedicated to tackling public crises need not only appear early on in evidence-based design processes. The examples of BI modifications or interventions shown in this Element are most prominent at the level of calibrations made to instruments during their on-the-ground implementation, at sub-jurisdictional levels. At the outset, such calibrations are shown in this context to be mainly information-based and utilise governance resources of nodality in support of regulatory measures issued at the state level.

With more long-term motivations for policy design and the inclusion of more sustained behavioural implications in managing a variety of sectors, governance resources beyond information-based tools become necessary. The principle described earlier for nudges engenders a trade-off for policy design between supporting quick reactions in the short term and embracing the complexity of human understanding and cognition in the long term. To induce long-term behavioural reflections, there is a need to design more 'thought provoking' nudges that also uphold public and individual agency (John, 2018; Strassheim, 2021). Over time, this deliberate turn of the behavioural policy revolution can require more organisational decisions to be made in order to scale up policy responses with changing governance contexts. For example, in a public health crisis this means being able to deploy BI resources for health monitoring and testing, ramping up social distancing efforts, and recognising the need to quickly augment and mobilise health resources during disease spikes. At the same time and within the same crisis, as shown in the global experience with COVID-19, more organisation and incentive-based decisions can concurrently be taken to sustain behavioural change, therefore reflecting more 'think' style BI design choices that favour deliberation and collaboration.

All in all, a rapidly growing array of opportunities exists with which to hypothesise about the evolving role of BI means in the policy design process (at times of crisis and otherwise). Firstly, is there a temporal nature to how BI means are designed initially as calibrations (micro-level) but lead to instances of collaboration and co-creation through more multi-instrument policy mixes and programmes (meso-level) over time? Is there an implication of causality between the design of procedural elements (e.g., establishing analytical behavioural insights units, project-specific taskforces and commissions) and substantive elements (e.g., adjustments made to vaccination messaging) of particular policy instrument mixes in policy sectors that have become most aligned with behavioural research? Secondly, are there 'orders' to which combination of governance resources are necessitated by the design of BI policy mechanisms, and do these relate to the suggested temporal trajectory of their diversity? Thirdly, how do these concerns of temporality and governance resources in BI tool design reflect different policy capacities that must be activated at the operational, programme and, eventually, system-wide levels of policy design? Finally, past and potential limitations of BI require a critical discussion and an adjusted outlook for their application. This is especially relevant in the light of recent criticisms levelled at BI in several instances around the world: from publication bias, failure to reach the necessary scale and flawed assumptions to neglect of social context and ethical concerns, among others (Hallsworth, 2023). These limitations warrant a deeper collaboration between various actors and across policy communities to ensure that BI means are implemented as part of a suite of policies without placing too much confidence in any one measure.

More completely, is the rise of behavioural policy tools spurring an equal shift in the work of policy design?

References

Abaluck, J., Kwong, L. H., Styczynski, A., et al. (2022). Impact of community masking on COVID-19: A cluster-randomized trial in Bangladesh. *Science*, *375*(6577), 1–13.

Abdukadirov, S. (2016). *Nudge theory in action: Behavioral design in policy and markets*. Springer.

Adams, R., Bessant, J., & Phelps, R. (2006). Innovation management measurement: A review. *International Journal of Management Reviews*, *8*(1), 21–47. https://doi.org/10.1111/j.1468-2370.2006.00119.x

Adner, R., & Helfat, C. E. (2003). Corporate effects and dynamic managerial capabilities. *Strategic Management Journal*, *24*(10), 1011–1025. https://doi.org/10.1002/smj.331

Afif, Z., Islan, W. W., Calvo-Gonzalez, O., & Dalton, A. (2019). *Behavioral science around the world: Profiles of 10 countries*. World Bank. https://documents1.worldbank.org/curated/en/710771543609067500/pdf/132610-REVISED-00-COUNTRY-PROFILES-dig.pd

Ahuja, G., Lampert, C. M., & Tandon, V. (2008). Moving beyond Schumpeter: Management research on the determinants of technological innovation. *Academy of Management Annals*, *2*(1), 1–98. https://doi.org/10.5465/19416520802211446

Aiken, M., & Hage, J. (1971). The organic organization and innovation. *Sociology*, *5*(1), 63–82. https://doi.org/10.1177/003803857100500105

Alemanno, A., & Sibony, A. L. (Eds.). (2015). *Nudge and the law: A European perspective*. Bloomsbury Publishing.

Andersen, D. F., & Dawes, S. S. (1991). *Government information management: A primer and casebook*. Prentice Hall.

Asian Development Bank. (2017). Behaviour change communication: If you build it, they may not come. *Asian Development Blog*, 18 December.

Atuahene-Gima, K. (2003). The effects of centrifugal and centripetal forces on product development speed and quality: How does problem solving matter? *Academy of Management Journal*, *46*(3), 359–373. https://doi.org/10.2307/30040629

Auld, G., Balboa, C., Bernstein, S., et al. (2009). The emergence of non-state market-driven (NSDM) global environmental governance. In M. A. Delmas & O. R. Young (Eds.), *Governance for the environment: New perspectives* (pp. 183–218). Cambridge University Press.

Baer, J. (1998). The case for domain specificity of creativity. *Creativity Research Journal, 11*(2), 173–177. https://doi.org/10.1207/s15326934crj1102_7

Baldridge, J. V., & Burnham, R. A. (1975). Organizational innovation: Individual, organizational, and environmental impacts. *Administrative Science Quarterly, 20*(2), 165–176. https://doi.org/10.2307/2391692

Bali, A. S., Howlett, M., Lewis, J. M., & Ramesh, M. (2021). Procedural policy tools in theory and practice. *Policy and Society, 40*(3), 295–311. https://doi.org/10.1080/14494035.2021.1965379

Ball, S., & Feitsma, J. (2020). The boundaries of behavioural insights: observations from two ethnographic studies. *Evidence & Policy, 16*(4), 559–577.

Ball, S., & Head, B. W. (2021). Behavioural insights teams in practice: Nudge missions and methods on trial. *Policy & Politics, 49*(1), 105–120. https://doi.org/10.1332/030557320X15840777045205

Ball, S., Hiscox, M., & Oliver, T. (2017). Starting a behavioural insights team: Three lessons from the Behavioural Economics Team of the Australian Government. *Journal of Behavioral Economics for Policy, 1*(Special Issue), 21–26.

Banerjee, A., Alsan, M., Breza, E., et al. (2020). Messages on COVID-19 prevention in India increased symptoms reporting and adherence to preventive behaviors among 25 million recipients with similar effects on non-recipient members of their communities (No. w27496). National Bureau of Economic Research.

Banerjee, S., & John, P. (2021). Nudge plus: Incorporating reflection into behavioral public policy. *Behavioural Public Policy, 8*(1), 69–84.

Barney, J. (1991). Firm resources and sustained competitive advantage. *Journal of Management, 17*(1), 99–120. https://doi.org/10.1177/014920639101700108

Battaglio Jr, R. P., Belardinelli, P., Bellé, N., & Cantarelli, P. (2019). Behavioral public administration ad fontes: A synthesis of research on bounded rationality, cognitive biases, and nudging in public organizations. *Public Administration Review, 79*(3), 304–320.

Bavel, J. J. V., Baicker, K., Boggio, P. S . . . & Willer, R. (2020). Using social and behavioural science to support COVID-19 pandemic response. *Nature Human Behaviour, 4*, 460–471.

Bechky, B. A. (2003). Object lessons: Workplace artifacts as representations of occupational jurisdiction. *American Journal of Sociology, 109*(3), 720–752. https://doi.org/10.1086/379527

Bemelmans-Videc, M.-L., Rist, R. C., & Vedung, E. O. (2011). *Carrots, sticks, and sermons: Policy instruments and their evaluation* (Vol. 1). Transaction Publishers.

Benartzi, S., Beshears, J., Milkman, K. L., et al. (2017). Should governments invest more in nudging? *Psychological Science, 28*(8), 1041–1055.

Bernstein, S. (2001). *The compromise of liberal environmentalism.* Columbia University Press.

Bernstein, S., & Cashore, B. (2000). Globalization, four paths of internationalization and domestic policy change: the case of ecoforestry in British Columbia, Canada. *Canadian Journal of Political Science/Revue canadienne de science politique, 33*(1), 67–99.

Bernstein, S., & Cashore, B. (2012). Complex global governance and domestic policies: Four pathways of influence. *International Affairs, 88*(3), 585–604.

Bobrow, D. B., & Dryzek, J. S. (1987). *Policy analysis by design.* University of Pittsburgh Press.

Bovens, L. (2009). The ethics of nudge. In T. Grüne-Yanoff & S. O. Hansson (Eds.), *Preference change: Approaches from philosophy, economics and psychology* (pp. 207–219). Springer.

Brenton, S., Baekkeskov, E., & Hannah, A. (2023). Policy capacity: Evolving theory and missing links. *Policy Studies, 44*(3), 297–315.

Brondizio, E. S., Ostrom, E., & Young, O. R. (2009). Connectivity and the governance of multilevel social-ecological systems: The role of social capital. *Annual Review of Environment and Resources, 34*, 253–278.

Capano, G. (2020). Studying public policy: A mechanistic perspective. In G. Capano & M. Howlett (Eds.), *A Modern Guide to Public Policy* (pp. 112–130). Edward Elgar Publishing.

Capano, G., & Engeli, I. (2022). Using instrument typologies in comparative research: Conceptual and methodological trade-offs. *Journal of Comparative Policy Analysis: Research and Practice, 24*(2), 99–116.

Capano, G., & Howlett, M. (2020). The knowns and unknowns of policy instrument analysis: Policy tools and the current research agenda on policy mixes. *Sage Open, 10*(1). https://doi.org/10.1177/2158244019 900568

Carlile, P. R. (2004). Transferring, translating, and transforming: An integrative framework for managing knowledge across boundaries. *Organization Science, 15*(5), 555–568. https://doi.org/10.1287/orsc.1040.0094

Carlsson, F., Gravert, C., Johansson-Stenman, O., & Kurz, V. (2021). The use of green nudges as an environmental policy instrument. *Review of Environmental Economics and Policy, 15*(2), 216–237.

Carter, L., & Bélanger, F. (2005). The utilization of e-government services: Citizen trust, innovation and acceptance factors. *Information Systems Journal, 15*(1), 5–25.

Cashore, B., Bernstein, S., Humphreys, D., et al. (2019). Designing stakeholder learning dialogues for effective global governance. *Policy and Society, 38*(1), 118–147.

Ciriolo, E., Lourenço, J. S., & Almeida, S. R. (2019). The application of behavioural insights to policy in Europe. In H. Straßheim & S. Beck (Eds.), *Handbook of behavioural change and public policy* (pp. 102–121). Edward Elgar Publishing.

Clark, K. B., & Fujimoto, T. (1991). *Product development performance: Strategy, organization, and management in the world auto industry.* Harvard Business Press.

Cohen, N., & Aviram, N. F. (2021). Street-level bureaucrats and policy entrepreneurship: When implementers challenge policy design. *Public Administration, 99*(3), 427–438.

Cohen, W. M., & Levinthal, D. A. (1990). Absorptive capacity: A new perspective on learning and innovation. *Administrative Science Quarterly, 35*(1), 128–152. https://doi.org/10.2307/2393553

Damanpour, F. (1991). Organizational innovation: A meta-analysis of effects of determinants and moderators. *Academy of Management Journal, 34*(3), 555–590. https://doi.org/10.2307/256406

Damanpour, F., Chiu, H., & Wischnevsky, J. (2009). Organizational complexity, resources and the adoption of management innovations: The influence of adoption process. European Academy of Management Conference, Liverpool.

Damanpour, F., & Schneider, M. (2006). Phases of the adoption of innovation in organizations: Effects of environment, organization and top managers. *British Journal of Management, 17*(3), 215–236. https://doi.org/10.1111/j.1467-8551.2006.00498.x

Datta, S., & Mullainathan, S. (2014). Behavioral design: A new approach to development policy. *Review of Income and Wealth, 60*(1), 7–35.

Dawes, S. S. (1996). Interagency information sharing: Expected benefits, manageable risks. *Journal of Policy Analysis and Management, 15*(3), 377–394.

Deaton, A., & Cartwright, N. (2018). Understanding and misunderstanding randomized controlled trials. *Social Science & Medicine, 210*, 2–21.

Debnath, R., & Bardhan, R. (2020). India nudges to contain COVID-19 pandemic: A reactive public policy analysis using machine-learning based topic modelling. *PloS One, 15*(9), e0238972. https://doi.org/10.1371/journal.pone.0238972

de Ridder, D., Feitsma, J., van den Hoven, M., et al. (2020). Simple nudges that are not so easy. *Behavioural Public Policy*, 1–19.

de Souza Leão, L., & Eyal, G. (2019). The rise of randomized controlled trials (RCTs) in international development in historical perspective. *Theory and Society, 48*, 383–418.

Detenber, B. H. (2021). Nudging in Singapore: Current implementation in three key areas. *Journal of Asian Economic Integration, 3*(1), 74–92. https://doi .org/10.1177/2631684620982776

Dolowitz, D. P., & Marsh, D. (2000). Learning from abroad: The role of policy transfer in contemporary policy-making. *Governance, 13*(1), 5–23. https:// doi.org/10.1111/0952-1895.00121

Dougherty, D. (1992). Interpretive barriers to successful product innovation in large firms. *Organization Science, 3*(2), 179–202. https://doi.org/10.1287/ orsc.3.2.179

Dougherty, D., & Dunne, D. D. (2012). Digital science and knowledge boundaries in complex innovation. *Organization Science, 23*(5), 1428–1447. https://doi.org/10.1287/orsc.1110.0700

DPM&C Australia. (2023). *BETA in 2022*. https://behaviouraleconomics.pmc .gov.au/blog/beta-2022

Durose, C., & Richardson, L. (2016). *Designing public policy for co-production*. Policy Press.

Edmondson, A. C., & Nembhard, I. M. (2009). Product development and learning in project teams: The challenges are the benefits. *Journal of Product Innovation Management, 26*(2), 123–138. https://doi.org/10.1111/ j.1540-5885.2009.00341.x

Einfeld, C., & Blomkamp, E. (2022). Nudge and co-design: Complementary or contradictory approaches to policy innovation? *Policy Studies, 43*(5), 901–919. https://doi.org/10.1080/01442872.2021.1879036

Eisenhardt, K. M., & Martin, J. A. (2000). Dynamic capabilities: What are they? *Strategic Management Journal, 21*(10–11), 1105–1121. https:// doi.org/10.1002/1097-0266(200010/11)21:10/11<1105::AID-SMJ133>3 .0.CO;2-E

Ekhardt, F., & Wieding, J. (2016). Nudging and environmental law. In K. Mathis & A. Tor (Eds.), *Nudging: Possibilities, limitations and applications in European law and economics*, (pp. 247–262). Springer.

Environmental Policy Committee (EPOC). (2017). Behavioural insights for environmentally relevant policies: Review of experiences from OECD countries and beyond. OECD Environment Directorate ENV/EPOC/ WPIEEP(2016)15/FINAL, JT03410762.

Ericsson, K. A., & Charness, N. (1994). Expert performance: Its structure and acquisition. *American Psychologist, 49*(8), 725–747. https://doi.org/10.1037/ 0003-066X.49.8.725

Ewert, B. (2020). Moving beyond the obsession with nudging individual behaviour: Towards a broader understanding of Behavioural Public Policy. *Public Policy and Administration, 35*(3), 337–360.

Ewert, B., & Loer, K. (2021). Advancing behavioural public policies: In pursuit of a more comprehensive concept. *Policy & Politics, 49*(1), 25–47.

Ewert, B., Loer, K., & Thomann, E. (2021). Beyond nudge: Advancing the state-of-the-art of behavioural public policy and administration. *Policy & Politics, 49*(1), 3–23.

Feitsma, J. N. P. (2018). The behavioural state: Critical observations on technocracy and psychocracy. *Policy Sciences, 51*(3), 387–410.

Feitsma, J. (2019). Brokering behaviour change: The work of behavioural insights experts in government. *Policy & Politics, 47*(1), 37–56.

Feitsma, J., & Schillemans, T. (2019). Behaviour experts in government: From newcomers to professionals? In H. Straßheim & S. Beck (Eds.), *Handbook of behavioural change and public policy* (pp. 122–137). Edward Elgar Publishing. https://doi.org/10.4337/9781785367854.00015

Feitsma, J., & Whitehead, M. (2022). Bounded interdisciplinarity: Critical interdisciplinary perspectives on context and evidence in behavioural public policies. *Behavioural Public Policy, 6*(3), 358–384.

Frambach, R. T., & Schillewaert, N. (2002). Organizational innovation adoption: A multi-level framework of determinants and opportunities for future research. *Journal of Business Research, 55*(2), 163–176. https://doi.org/10.1016/S0148-2963(00)00152-1

Galizzi, M. M. (2017). Behavioral aspects of policy formulation: Experiments, behavioral insights, nudges. In M. Howlett, I. Mukherjee, & S. Fraser (Eds.), *Handbook of policy formulation* (pp. 410–430). Edward Elgar Publishing.

Garrard, J., Rose, G., & Lo, S. K. (2008). Promoting transportation cycling for women: The role of bicycle infrastructure. *Preventive Medicine, 46*(1), 55–59. https://doi.org/10.1016/j.ypmed.2007.07.010

Giest, S., & Mukherjee, I. (2018). Behavioral instruments in renewable energy and the role of big data: A policy perspective. *Energy Policy, 123*, 360–366.

Gil-Garcia, J. R., & Martinez-Moyano, I. J. (2007). Understanding the evolution of e-government: The influence of systems of rules on public sector dynamics. *Government Information Quarterly, 24*(2), 266–290.

Gilabert, P., & Lawford-Smith, H. (2012). Political feasibility: A conceptual exploration. *Political Studies, 60*(4), 809–825.

Givoni, M., Macmillen, J., Banister, D., & Feitelson, E. (2013). From policy measures to policy packages. *Transport Reviews, 33*(1), 1–20.

Gopalakrishnan, S., & Damanpour, F. (1997). A review of innovation research in economics, sociology and technology management. *Omega, 25*(1), 15–28. https://doi.org/10.1016/S0305-0483(96)00043-6

Gopalan, M., & Pirog, M. A. (2017). Applying behavioral insights in policy analysis: Recent trends in the United States. *Policy Studies Journal, 45*(S1), S82–S114.

Grant, R. M. (1996). Prospering in dynamically-competitive environments: Organizational capability as knowledge integration. *Organization Science, 7*(4), 375–387. https://doi.org/10.1287/orsc.7.4.375

Gravert, C., & Shreedhar, G. (2022). Effective carbon taxes need green nudges. *Nature Climate Change, 12*(12), 1073–1074.

Grüne-Yanoff, T., & Hertwig, R. (2016). Nudge versus boost: How coherent are policy and theory? *Minds and Machines, 26*(1), 149–183.

Hallsworth, M. (2023). A manifesto for applying behavioural science. *Nature Human Behaviour, 7*, 310–322.

Hallsworth, M., & Kirkman, E. (2020). *Behavioral insights*. MIT Press.

Halpern, D. (2015a). Can 'nudging' change behaviour? Using 'behavioural insights' to improve program redesign. In J. Wanna, H.-A. Lee, & S. Yates (Eds.), *Managing under austerity, delivering under pressure* (pp. 165–179). ANU Press.

Halpern, D. (2015b). *Inside the nudge unit: How small changes can make a big difference*. Random House.

Halpern, D. (2015c). The rise of psychology in policy: The UK's de facto Council of Psychological Science Advisers. *Perspectives on Psychological Science, 10*(6), 768–771.

Hameed, M. A., & Counsell, S. (2014). Establishing relationships between innovation characteristics and IT innovation adoption in organisations: A meta-analysis approach. *International Journal of Innovation Management, 18*(1), 1450007.

Hameed, M. A., Counsell, S., & Swift, S. (2012). A meta-analysis of relationships between organizational characteristics and IT innovation adoption in organizations. *Information & Management, 49*(5), 218–232. https://doi.org/10.1016/j.im.2012.05.002

Hartley, K., & Jarvis, D. S. (2020). Policymaking in a low-trust state: Legitimacy, state capacity, and responses to COVID-19 in Hong Kong. *Policy and Society, 39*(3), 403–423.

Hausman, D. M., & Welch, B. (2010). Debate: To nudge or not to nudge. *Journal of Political Philosophy, 18*(1), 123–136.

Haynes, L., Service, O., Goldacre, B., & Torgerson, D. (2012). *Test, learn, adapt: Developing public policy with randomised controlled trials* (SSRN Scholarly Paper No. 2131581). https://doi.org/10.2139/ssrn.2131581

Helfat, C. E., & Martin, J. A. (2015). Dynamic managerial capabilities: Review and assessment of managerial impact on strategic change. *Journal of Management, 41*(5), 1281–1312. https://doi.org/10.1177/01492063145 61301

Hertwig, R., & Grüne-Yanoff, T. (2017). Nudging and boosting: Steering or empowering good decisions. *Perspectives on Psychological Science, 12*(6), 973–986.

Hill, M., & Varone, F. (2016). *The public policy process.* Taylor & Francis.

Holland, S., Gaston, K., & Gomes, J. (2000). Critical success factors for cross-functional teamwork in new product development. *International Journal of Management Reviews, 2*(3), 231–259. https://doi.org/10.1111/1468-2370 .00040

Hood, C. (2007). Intellectual obsolescence and intellectual makeovers: Reflections on the tools of government after two decades. *Governance, 20* (1), 127–144.

Hood, C., & Margetts, H. (2007). *The tools of government in the digital age.* Bloomsbury Publishing.

Howieson, J., Lawley, M., & Selen, W. (2014). New product development in small food enterprises. *Journal of New Business Ideas & Trends, 12*(1), 11–26.

Howlett, M. (2000). Managing the 'hollow state': Procedural policy instruments and modern governance. *Canadian Public Administration/Administration Publique Du Canada, 43*(4), 412–431. https://doi.org/10.1111/j.1754-7121.2000.tb01152.x

Howlett, M. (2018). Matching policy tools and their targets: Beyond nudges and utility maximisation in policy design. *Policy & Politics, 46*(1), 101–124.

Howlett, M., & Leong, C. (2022). What is behavioral in policy studies? How far has the discipline moved beyond traditional utilitarianism? *Journal of Behavioral Public Administration, 5*(1).

Howlett, M., & Ramesh, M. (1998). Policy subsystem configurations and policy change: Operationalizing the postpositivist analysis of the politics of the policy process. *Policy Studies Journal, 26*(3), 466–481. https://doi.org/ 10.1111/j.1541-0072.1998.tb01913.x

Howlett, M., & Ramesh, M. (2016). Achilles' heels of governance: Critical capacity deficits and their role in governance failures: The Achilles heel of governance. *Regulation & Governance, 10*(4), 301–313. https://doi.org/10 .1111/rego.12091

Howlett, M., Ramesh, M., & Capano, G. (2020). Policy-makers, policy-takers and policy tools: Dealing with behavioural issues in policy design. *Journal of Comparative Policy Analysis: Research and Practice, 22*(6), 487–497.

Howlett, M., Ramesh, M., & Perl, A. (2009). *Studying public policy: Policy cycles and policy subsystems* (Vol. 3). Oxford University Press.

John, P. (2013). All tools are informational now: How information and persuasion define the tools of government. *Policy & Politics, 41*(4), 605–620.

John, P. (2018). *How far to nudge? Assessing behavioural public policy.* Edward Elgar Publishing.

John, P., & Blume, T. (2018). How best to nudge taxpayers? The impact of message simplification and descriptive social norms on payment rates in a central London local authority. *Journal of Behavioral Public Administration, 1*(1). https://doi.org/10.30636/jbpa.11.10

John, P., Cotterill, S., Moseley, A., et al. (2020). *Nudge, nudge, think, think: Experimenting with ways to change citizen behaviour.* Manchester University Press.

John, P., & Stoker, G. (2019). Rethinking the role of experts and expertise in behavioural public policy. *Policy & Politics, 47*(2), 209–226.

Jones, R., Pykett, J., & Whitehead, M. (2013). *Changing behaviours: On the rise of the psychological state.* Edward Elgar Publishing.

Jones, S., Head, B., & Ferguson, M. (2021). In search of policy innovation: Behavioural Insights Teams in Australia and New Zealand. *Australian Journal of Public Administration, 80*(3), 435–452. https://doi.org/10.1111/1467-8500.12478

Kaplan, S., Milde, J., & Cowan, R. S. (2017). Symbiont practices in boundary spanning: Bridging the cognitive and political divides in interdisciplinary research. *Academy of Management Journal, 60*(4), 1387–1414. https://doi.org/10.5465/amj.2015.0809

Karaman Akgul, A., & Gozlu, S. (2015). The role of organizational resources and market competitiveness in innovativeness. *Journal of Business, Economics and Finance, 4*(1), 166–184. http://doi.org/10.17261/Pressacademia.2015110016

Kellogg, K. C. (2014). Brokerage professions and implementing reform in an age of experts. *American Sociological Review, 79*(5), 912–941. https://doi.org/10.1177/0003122414544734

Kimberly, J. R., & Evanisko, M. J. (1981). Organizational innovation: The influence of individual, organizational, and contextual factors on hospital adoption of technological and administrative innovations. *Academy of Management Journal, 24*(4), 689–713. https://psycnet.apa.org/doi/10.2307/256170

Kirkman, D. M. (2012). Social enterprises: A multi-level framework of the innovation adoption process. *Innovation, 14*(1), 143–155. https://doi.org/10.5172/impp.2012.14.1.143

Kislov, R., Hodgson, D., & Boaden, R. (2016). Professionals as knowledge brokers: The limits of authority in healthcare collaboration. *Public Administration, 94*(2), 472–489. https://doi.org/10.1111/padm.12227

Klein, K. J., & Sorra, J. S. (1996). The challenge of innovation implementation. *The Academy of Management Review, 21*(4), 1055–1080. https://doi.org/10.2307/259164

Klijn, E.-H., Koppenjan, J., & Termeer, K. (1995). Managing networks in the public sector: A theoretical study of management strategies in policy networks. *Public Administration, 73*(3), 437–454.

Knetsch, J. (2012). Behavioural economics, policy analysis and the design of regulatory reform. In D. Low (Ed.), *Behavioural economics and policy design: Examples from Singapore* (pp. 161–182). World Scientific.

Knight, C., & Lyall, C. (2013). Knowledge brokers: The role of intermediaries in producing research impact. *Evidence & Policy, 9*(3), 309–316. https://doi.org/10.1332/174426413X671941

Kok, P. S. (n.d.). Nudges: Why, how and what next? *Ethos, 17*, 6–15. https://knowledge.csc.gov.sg/ethos-issue-17/nudges-why-how-what-next/

Kosters, M., & Van der Heijden, J. (2015). From mechanism to virtue: Evaluating Nudge theory. *Evaluation, 21*(3), 276–291.

Krueger, J. I., & Funder, D. C. (2004). Towards a balanced social psychology: Causes, consequences, and cures for the problem-seeking approach to social behavior and cognition. *Behavioral and Brain Sciences, 27*(3), 313–327.

Kuehnhanss, C. R. (2019). The challenges of behavioural insights for effective policy design. *Policy and Society, 38*(1), 14–40.

Kulkarni, D., & Simon, H. A. (1988). The processes of scientific discovery: The strategy of experimentation. *Cognitive Science, 12*(2), 139–175. https://doi.org/10.1207/s15516709cog1202_1

Kwon, T. H., & Zmud, R. W. (1987). Unifying the fragmented models of information systems implementation. In R. J. Boland & R. A. Hirschheim (Eds.), *Critical issues in information systems research* (pp. 227–251). Wiley.

Lee, K. Y. (2012). *From third world to first: The Singapore story, 1965–2000.* Marshall Cavendish International Asia Pte Ltd.

Lehner, M., Mont, O., & Heiskanen, E. (2016). Nudging: A promising tool for sustainable consumption behaviour? *Journal of Cleaner Production, 134*, 166–177.

Lepenies, R., & Małecka, M. (2015). The institutional consequences of nudging: Nudges, politics, and the law. *Review of Philosophy and Psychology, 6*(3), 427–437.

Lewin, K. (1952). Group decision and social change. In T. Newcombe & E. Hartley, *Readings in social psychology* (pp. 197–211). Henry Holt.

Lewis, L. K., & Seibold, D. R. (1993). Innovation modification during intraorganizational adoption. *The Academy of Management Review, 18*(2), 322–354. https://doi.org/10.2307/258762

Lodge, M., & Wegrich, K. (2016). The rationality paradox of nudge: Rational tools of government in a world of bounded rationality. *Law & Policy, 38*(3), 250–267.

Low, D. (2011). *Behavioural economics and policy design: Examples from Singapore.* World Scientific.

Lunn, P. D. (2012). Behavioural economics and policymaking: Learning from the early adopters. *The Economic and Social Review, 43*(3), 423–449.

Maddix, N. (2017). What is the future of behavioral research and large-scale nudges? Five practical tips. *Behavioural Economics*, 31 October. www.behavioraleconomics.com/future-behavioral-research-nudges/

Mani, A. (2021). Experimental evidence, scaling and public policy: A perspective from developing countries. *Behavioural Public Policy, 5*(1), 103–111.

Maor, M. (2020). Policy over-and under-design: An information quality perspective. *Policy Sciences, 53*(3), 395–411.

Margetts, H., & Hood, C. (2016). Tools approaches. In B. G. Peters & P. Zittoun (Eds.), *Contemporary Approaches to Public Policy: Theories, Controversies and Perspectives* (pp. 133–154). Palgrave Macmillan.

Marteau, T. M., Ogilvie, D., Roland, M., et al. (2011). Judging nudging: Can nudging improve population health? *BMJ, 342*, d228. https://doi.org/10.1136/bmj.d228

Matta, V., Koonce, D., & Jeyaraj, A. (2012). Initiation, experimentation, implementation of innovations: The case for radio frequency identification systems. *International Journal of Information Management, 32*(2), 164–174. https://doi.org/10.1016/j.ijinfomgt.2011.10.002

Mellström, C., & Johannesson, M. (2008). Crowding out in blood donation: was Titmuss right? *Journal of the European Economic Association, 6*(4), 845–863.

Meyer, M. (2010). The rise of the knowledge broker. *Science Communication, 32*(1), 118–127. https://doi.org/10.1177/1075547009359797

Mitnick, B. M. (1980). Incentive systems in environmental regulation. *Policy Studies Journal, 9*(3), 379–394.

Mont, O., Lehner, M., & Heiskanen, E. (2014). *Nudging: A tool for sustainable behaviour?* Naturvårdsverket.

Moodie, A. R. (2008). Australia: The healthiest country by 2020. *Medical Journal of Australia, 189*(10), 588–590.

Moseley, A. (2020). Nudging in public policy. In *Oxford research encyclopedia of politics*. https://oxfordre.com/politics/display/10.1093/acrefore/

9780190228637.001.0001/acrefore-9780190228637-e-949;jsessionid=
17364D96820DD9DDFBB7D0C279C72C4D?rskey=yWvNqs&
result=222

Moynihan, D. P. (2018). A great schism approaching? Towards a micro and
macro public administration: Towards a micro and macro public administration. *Journal of Behavioral Public Administration*, *1*(1). https://doi.org/
10.30636/jbpa.11.15

Mukherjee, I., & Bali, A. S. (2019). Policy effectiveness and capacity: two sides
of the design coin. *Policy Design and Practice*, *2*(2), 103–114.

Mukherjee, I., Coban, M. K., & Bali, A. S. (2021). Policy capacities and
effective policy design: A review. *Policy Sciences*, *54*(2), 243–268.

Mukherjee, I., & Giest, S. (2020). Behavioural insights teams (BITs) and policy
change: An exploration of impact, location, and temporality of policy advice.
Administration & Society, *52*(10), 1538–1561.

Mukherjee, I., & Mukherjee, N. (2018). Designing for sustainable outcomes:
Espousing behavioural change into co-production programmes. *Policy and
Society*, *37*(3), 326–346.

Mumford, M. D. (2000). Managing creative people: Strategies and tactics for
innovation. *Human Resource Management Review*, *10*(3), 313–351. https://
doi.org/10.1016/S1053-4822(99)00043-1

Nauwelaers, C., & Wintjes, R. (2008). Innovation policy, innovation in policy:
Policy learning within and across systems and clusters. In C. Nauwelaers &
R. Wintjes (Eds.), *Innovation Policy in Europe: Measurement and Strategy*
(pp. 225–268). Edward Elgar Publishing.

Nicolini, D., Mengis, J., & Swan, J. (2012). Understanding the role of objects in
cross-disciplinary collaboration. *Organization Science*, *23*(3), 612–629.
https://doi.org/10.1287/orsc.1110.0664

Nonaka, I. (1994). A dynamic theory of organizational knowledge creation.
Organization Science, *5*(1), 14–37. https://doi.org/10.1287/orsc.5.1.14

NSW Behavioural Insights Unit. (2020). *Behavioural insights*. www.nsw.gov
.au/behavioural-insights-unit

OECD (2017). *Behavioural insights and public policy: Lessons from around the
world*. OECD Publishing. https://doi.org/10.1787/9789264270480-en

Ohly, S., Sonnentag, S., & Pluntke, F. (2006). Routinization, work characteristics and their relationships with creative and proactive behaviors. *Journal
of Organizational Behavior*, *27*(3), 257–279. https://doi.org/10.1002/
job.376

Okhuysen, G. A., & Eisenhardt, K. M. (2002). Integrating knowledge in groups:
How formal interventions enable flexibility. *Organization Science*, *13*(4),
370–386. https://doi.org/10.1287/orsc.13.4.370.2947

Oliver, A. (2015). Nudging, shoving, and budging: Behavioural economic-informed policy. *Public Administration, 93*(3), 700–714.

Ostrom, E. (2000). Collective action and the evolution of social norms. *Journal of Economic Perspectives, 14*(3), 137–158.

Pal, L. A. (1992). *Public policy analysis: An introduction.* Nelson Education Canada.

Penrose, E. T. (1959). *The theory of the growth of the firm.* John Wiley.

Penrose, E., & Penrose, E. T. (2009). *The theory of the growth of the firm.* Oxford University Press.

Pershina, R., Soppe, B., & Thune, T. M. (2019). Bridging analog and digital expertise: Cross-domain collaboration and boundary-spanning tools in the creation of digital innovation. *Research Policy, 48*(9), 103819. https://doi.org/10.1016/j.respol.2019.103819

Peters, B. G., Capano, G., Howlett, M., et al. (2018). *Designing for policy effectiveness: Defining and understanding a concept.* Cambridge University Press.

Pichlak, M. (2016). The innovation adoption process: A multidimensional approach. *Journal of Management & Organization, 22*(4), 476–494. https://doi.org/10.1017/jmo.2015.52

Pichlak, M., & Bratnicki, M. (2011). The role of leadership in product innovation. *Management, 15*(1), 25–38.

Pierce, J. L., & Delbecq, A. L. (1977). Organization structure, individual attitudes and innovation. *The Academy of Management Review, 2*(1), 27–37. https://doi.org/10.2307/257602

Prajogo, D., & McDermott, C. M. (2014). Antecedents of service innovation in SMEs: Comparing the effects of external and internal factors. *Journal of Small Business Management, 52*(3), 521–540. https://doi.org/10.1111/jsbm.12047

Premkumar, G., & Roberts, M. (1999). Adoption of new information technologies in rural small businesses. *Omega, 27*(4), 467–484. https://doi.org/10.1016/S0305-0483(98)00071-1

Public Service Division. (2014). *Policy making tip: Nudge, not hove.* Challenge.

Rafiq, S., Salim, R., & Nielsen, I. (2016). Urbanization, openness, emissions, and energy intensity: A study of increasingly urbanized emerging economies. *Energy Economics, 56*, 20–28.

Rangone, N. (2018). Making law effective: Behavioural insights into compliance. *European Journal of Risk Regulation, 9*(3), 483–501.

Ravasi, D., & Verona, G. (2001). Organising the process of knowledge integration: The benefits of structural ambiguity. *Scandinavian Journal of Management, 17*(1), 41–66. https://doi.org/10.1016/S0956-5221(00)00032-4

Rawat, S. (2019). A bibliometric analysis of behavioural studies in economics and public policy journals. In H. Straßheim & S. Beck (Eds.), *Handbook of behavioural change and public policy* (pp. 49–62). Edward Elgar Publishing.

Richardson, L., & John, P. (2021). Co-designing behavioural public policy: Lessons from the field about how to 'nudge plus'. *Evidence & Policy, 17*(3), 405–422.

Roberts, E. B. (1988). What we've learned: Managing invention and innovation. *Research-Technology Management, 31*(1), 11–29. https://doi.org/10.1080/08956308.1988.11670497

Rogers, E. M. (1995). Diffusion of innovations: Modifications of a model for telecommunications. In M.-W. Stoetzer & A. Mahler (Eds.), *Die Diffusion von Innovationen in der Telekommunikation* (pp. 25–38). Springer Berlin Heidelberg. https://doi.org/10.1007/978-3-642-79868-9_2

Rose, N. (1998). *Inventing our selves: Psychology, power, and personhood.* Cambridge University Press.

Ruggeri, K. (2018). *Behavioral insights for public policy: Concepts and cases.* Routledge.

Saguin, K., Ramesh, M., & Howlett, M. (2018). Policy work and capacities in a developing country: Evidence from the Philippines. *Asia Pacific Journal of Public Administration, 40*(1), 1–22.

Salamon, L. M. (2000). The new governance and the tools of public action: An introduction. *Fordham Urban Law Journal, 28*(5), 1611–1674.

Schneider, A., & Ingram, H. (1990). Behavioral assumptions of policy tools. *The Journal of Politics, 52*(2), 510–529.

Scopelliti, I., Cillo, P., Busacca, B., & Mazursky, D. (2014). How do financial constraints affect creativity? Creativity under financial constraints. *Journal of Product Innovation Management, 31*(5), 880–893. https://doi.org/10.1111/jpim.12129

Seawright, J., & Gerring, J. (2008). Case selection techniques in case study research: A menu of qualitative and quantitative options. *Political Research Quarterly, 61*(2), 294–308.

Serafica, P. (n.d.). *Behavior change communication: If you build it, they may not come.* Asian Development Blog. Retrieved 23 May 2023, from https://blogs.adb.org/blog/behavior-change-communication-if-you-build-it-they-may-not-come

Sewerin, S., Cashore, B., & Howlett, M. (2022). New pathways to paradigm change in public policy: Combining insights from policy design, mix and feedback. *Policy & Politics, 50*(3), 442–459.

Shafir, E. (2013). *The behavioral foundations of public policy.* Princeton University Press.

Sidney, M. S. (2007). Policy formulation: design and tools. In F. Fischer, G. J. Miller, & M. S. Sidney (Eds.), *Handbook of public policy analysis: Theory, politics and methods* (pp. 79–87). CRC Taylor & Francis.

Simonton, D. K. (1988). Creativity, leadership, and chance. In R. J. Sternberg (Ed.), *The Nature of Creativity: Contemporary Psychological Perspectives* (pp. 386–426). Cambridge University Press.

Soon, K. P. (2017). Nudging: Why, how, what next? *Ethos, 17.* https://know ledge.csc.gov.sg/ethos-issue-17/nudges-why-how-what-next/

Sørensen, E., & Torfing, J. (2011). Enhancing collaborative innovation in the public sector. *Administration & Society, 43*(8), 842–868. https://doi.org/ 10.1177/0095399711418768

Star, S. L., & Griesemer, J. R. (1989). Institutional ecology, 'translations' and boundary objects: Amateurs and professionals in Berkeley's Museum of Vertebrate Zoology, 1907–39. *Social Studies of Science, 19*(3), 387–420. https://doi.org/10.1177/030631289019003001

Steg, L., Bolderdijk, J. W., Keizer, K., & Perlaviciute, G. (2014). An integrated framework for encouraging pro-environmental behaviour: The role of values, situational factors and goals. *Journal of Environmental Psychology, 38,* 104–115.

Straßheim, H. (2020). The rise and spread of behavioral public policy: An opportunity for critical research and self-reflection. *International Review of Public Policy, 2*(1), 115–128.

Straßheim, H. (2021). Who are behavioural public policy experts and how are they organised globally? *Policy & Politics, 49*(1), 69–86.

Straßheim, H., & Beck, S. (Eds.). (2019). *Handbook of behavioural change and public policy.* Edward Elgar Publishing.

Teece, D. J. (1992). Competition, cooperation, and innovation: Organizational arrangements for regimes of rapid technological progress. *Journal of Economic Behavior & Organization, 18*(1), 1–25.

Teece, D. J., Pisano, G., & Shuen, A. (1997). Dynamic capabilities and strategic management. *Strategic Management Journal, 18*(7), 509–533. https://doi .org/10.1002/(SICI)1097-0266(199708)18:7<509::AID-SMJ882>3.0.CO;2-Z

Thaler, R. H., & Sunstein, C. R. (2009). *Nudge: Improving decisions about health, wealth, and happiness.* Penguin.

Thierer, A. (2016). Failing better: What we learn by confronting risk and uncertainty. In S. Abdukadirov (Ed.), *Nudge theory in action: Behavioral design in policy and markets* (pp. 65–94). Palgrave Macmillan.

van Roekel, H., Giurge, L. M., Schott, C., & Tummers, L. (2023). Nudges can be both autonomy-preserving and effective: evidence from a survey and quasi-field experiment. *Behavioural Public Policy,* 1–24.

Van Ryzin, G. G. (2021). Nudging and muddling through. *Perspectives on Public Management and Governance, 4*(4), 339–345.

Walker, R. M., Jeanes, E. L., & Rowlands, R. O. (2001). *Managing public services innovation.* Policy Press.

Wan, C., Shen, G. Q., & Yu, A. (2015). Key determinants of willingness to support policy measures on recycling: A case study in Hong Kong. *Environmental Science & Policy, 54,* 409–418.

Wang, C. L., & Ahmed, P. K. (2007). Dynamic capabilities: A review and research agenda. *International Journal of Management Reviews, 9*(1), 31–51. https://doi.org/10.1111/j.1468-2370.2007.00201.x

Ward, V., House, A., & Hamer, S. (2009). Knowledge brokering: The missing link in the evidence to action chain? *Evidence & Policy, 5*(3), 267–279. https://doi.org/10.1332/174426409X463811

Whitehead, M., Jones, R., Lilley, R., et al. (2017). *Neuroliberalism: Behavioural government in the twenty-first century.* Routledge.

Weible, C. M. (2018). Instrument constituencies and the advocacy coalition framework: An essay on the comparisons, opportunities, and intersections. *Policy and Society, 37*(1), 59–73.

World Bank. (2014). *World development report 2015: Mind, society, and behavior.* The World Bank.

World Bank. (2019). Behavioral science around the world: Profiles of 10 countries (English). eMBeD brief. sWorld Bank Group.

Wu, X., Ramesh, M., & Howlett, M. (2015). Policy capacity: A conceptual framework for understanding policy competences and capabilities. *Policy and Society, 34*(3–4), 165–171. https://doi.org/10.1016/j.polsoc.2015.09.001

Yew, L. K. (2012). *From third world to first: The Singapore story, 1965–2000.* Marshall Cavendish International Asia Pte Ltd.

Zaltman, G., Duncan, R., & Holbek, J. (1973). *Innovations and organizations.* Wiley.

Acknowledgement

Ishani Mukherjee would like to thank the Lee Kong Chian Fellowship for supporting her contribution in this Element.

Cambridge Elements ≡

Public Policy

M. Ramesh

National University of Singapore (NUS)

M. Ramesh is UNESCO Chair on Social Policy Design at the Lee Kuan Yew School of Public Policy, NUS. His research focuses on governance and social policy in East and Southeast Asia, in addition to public policy institutions and processes. He has published extensively in reputed international journals. He is co-editor of *Policy and Society* and *Policy Design and Practice*.

Michael Howlett

Simon Fraser University, British Columbia

Michael Howlett is Burnaby Mountain Professor and Canada Research Chair (Tier1) in the Department of Political Science, Simon Fraser University. He specialises in public policy analysis, and resource and environmental policy. He is currently editor-in-chief of *Policy Sciences* and co-editor of the *Journal of Comparative Policy Analysis*, *Policy and Society* and *Policy Design and Practice*.

Xun WU

Hong Kong University of Science and Technology (Guangzhou)

Xun WU is currently a Professor at the Innovation, Policy and Entrepreneurship Thrust at the Society Hub of Hong Kong University of Science and Technology (Guangzhou). He is a policy scientist with a strong interest in the linkage between policy analysis and public management. Trained in engineering, economics, public administration, and policy analysis, his research seeks to make contribution to the design of effective public policies in dealing emerging policy challenges across Asian countries.

Judith Clifton

University of Cantabria

Judith Clifton is Professor of Economics at the University of Cantabria, Spain, and Editor-in-Chief of *Journal of Economic Policy Reform*. Her research interests include the determinants and consequences of public policy across a wide range of public services, from infrastructure to health, particularly in Europe and Latin America, as well as public banks, especially, the European Investment Bank. Most recently, she is principal investigator on the Horizon Europe Project GREENPATHS (www.greenpaths.info) on the just green transition.

Eduardo Araral

National University of Singapore (NUS)

Eduardo Araral specializes in the study of the causes and consequences of institutions for collective action and the governance of the commons. He is widely published in various journals and books and has presented in more than ninety conferences. Ed was a 2021–22 Fellow at the Center for Advanced Study of Behavioral Sciences, Stanford University. He has received more than US$6.6 million in external research grants as the lead or co-PI for public agencies and corporations. He currently serves as a Special Issue Editor (collective action, commons, institutions, governance) for World Development and is a member of the editorial boards of *Water Economics and Policy, World Development Sustainability, Water Alternatives* and the *International Journal of the Commons*.

About the Series

Elements in Public Policy is a concise and authoritative collection of assessments of the state of the art and future research directions in public policy research, as well as substantive new research on key topics. Edited by leading scholars in the field, the series is an ideal medium for reflecting on and advancing the understanding of critical issues in the public sphere. Collectively, the series provides a forum for broad and diverse coverage of all major topics in the field while integrating different disciplinary and methodological approaches.

Cambridge Elements $\equiv$

Public Policy

Printed in the United States
by Baker & Taylor Publisher Services